Horatio Hale

**An International Idiom**

A manual of the Oregon trade language

Horatio Hale

**An International Idiom**
*A manual of the Oregon trade language*

ISBN/EAN: 9783337019051

Printed in Europe, USA, Canada, Australia, Japan

Cover: Foto ©ninafisch / pixelio.de

More available books at **www.hansebooks.com**

*AN INTERNATIONAL IDIOM.*

A MANUAL OF THE

# OREGON TRADE LANGUAGE,

OR

"CHINOOK JARGON."

By HORATIO HALE, M.A., F.R.S.C.,

MEMBER OF THE AMERICAN PHILOSOPHICAL SOCIETY; OF THE ANTHROPOLOGICAL INSTITUTE OF GREAT BRITAIN AND IRELAND; OF THE ANTHROPOLOGICAL SOCIETIES OF VIENNA AND WASHINGTON; OF THE CANADIAN INSTITUTE, ETC.

*Author of " Ethnography and Philology of the U.S. Exploring Expedition " The Iroquois Book of Rites," &c.*

LONDON:

WHITTAKER & CO., White Hart Street,

PATERNOSTER SQUARE.

1890.

CHISWICK PRESS:—C. WHITTINGHAM AND CO., TOOKS COURT,
CHANCERY LANE.

# PREFATORY NOTE.

THE following treatise was designed to form part of a larger volume of linguistics, the work of several con-

### CORRIGENDA.

P. 10, line 10, for *q* read *g*.
,, ,, 12 from below under "Jargon," for *ikeh'* read *tikeh'*.
,, ,, 6 ,, ,, "Chinook," for *taghka* read *iaghka*.

best results, among populations in various stages of civilization, speaking more than twenty distinct languages, and diffused over a territory nearly half as large as Europe.

*Extract from the "Introduction to the Study of the Human Races;" by A. de Quatrefages. Part II., p. 603. (Paris, 1889.)*

"The formation of these new languages deserves to attract the attention of linguists; and it will be fortunate if the example given by Mr. Hale should arouse their interest on this point. That eminent anthropologist has found in Oregon and north of that country a sort of *lingua franca*, which, born at first of the necessities of commerce, is to-day employed almost solely by many individuals. This idiom has already its vocabulary, its rules, its grammar. The elements composing it are borrowed from four languages—two American (Nootka and Chinook) and two European (French and English). A certain number of words have been formed by onomatopœia; and the language admits the formation of compound words to supply the deficiencies of its vocabulary."

# CONTENTS.

|  | PAGE |
|---|---|
| THE OREGON TRADE LANGUAGE | 1 |
| ITS ORIGIN AND COMPOSITION | 3 |
| ORTHOGRAPHY AND PRONUNCIATION | 9 |
| GRAMMAR | 12 |
| PAST AND FUTURE OF THE LANGUAGE | 19 |
| SONGS | 24 |
| HYMNS | 26 |
| A MISSIONARY SERMON | 28 |
| THE LORD'S PRAYER | 37 |
| DICTIONARY :— | |
|     TRADE LANGUAGE AND ENGLISH | 39 |
|     ENGLISH AND TRADE LANGUAGE | 53 |

# THE OREGON TRADE LANGUAGE,

OR,

## "CHINOOK JARGON."

THE interest recently awakened in the subject of an international language has given a new importance to a study originally made for purely scientific purposes more than forty years ago. As a member of the United States Exploring Expedition, which surveyed a portion of the western coast of North America in 1841, I undertook the charge of giving an account of the ethnology of Oregon. This name, now restricted to a single State, was then applied to an unorganized and undefined territory, a "debatable land," as it might have been truly styled, which stretched northward between the Rocky Mountains and the Pacific, from what was then the Mexican province of California to the as yet undetermined limit of the British possessions. My opportunities, however, did not allow me to extend my researches much to the north of the present southern boundary of those possessions. Within the space thus limited—a space larger than France—there was ample work to occupy an ethnologist for a much longer time than I was enabled to devote to the task.

On commencing that work I encountered at once two remarkable phenomena, the one of which added greatly to the labour of the inquirer, while the other afforded an equally notable and unexpected help. The great obstacle, as it seemed, and indeed was—though it has proved ultimately the source of most valuable gains to philological science—was the surprising number of distinct languages which were found to exist within this limited area. Twelve of these languages were distinct, not in the sense in which the Spanish differs from the Italian, but in the sense in which the Hebrew differs from the English; that is, they belonged to separate linguistic stocks, utterly dissimilar in words and in grammar. Furthermore, several of these stocks were split up into dialects, which sometimes differed so widely that the speakers of one of them could not be understood by the speakers of another. To work one's way through this maze of idioms, many of them exceedingly harsh and obscure in pronunciation and intricate in construction, to a correct classification of tribes and stocks, seemed likely to be a work of no small difficulty.

But the perplexity was lightened and almost removed by an aid which, as it appeared, this very difficulty had called into being. The needs of commerce, that had suddenly arisen with the advent of the foreign traders, required some common medium of communication. The "Trade Language," which came afterwards to be known as the "Chinook Jargon," grew into existence. As finally developed, it has become really an "international speech," widely diffused among the fifty tribes of Oregon, British Columbia, and Alaska, and of inestimable service, not only to commerce, but to science, to missionary efforts, and to the convenience of travellers. Nor were even these the chief benefits which have sprung from it. A well-informed writer, Mr. James Deans, in a recent article relating to the tribes of British Columbia, gives some striking evidence on this point. "Pride and ignorance of the languages of their neighbours were," he tells us, "the principal causes of the wars and ill-feeling between the various nations. For example, some ill-timed joke would, through ignorance on the part of the members of another tribe, be construed into an insult, which their pride would not allow to go unpunished." This root of infinite mischief has been extirpated, he informs us, by that "trade language or jargon, the Chinook," which "the traders found it necessary to create,"—"than which," he adds, "I know nothing that has done so much to civilize our native races. It stimulated friendly intercourse between tribes, by enabling them to converse with each other,—whence sworn foes became lasting friends."[1]

The origin and character of this interesting speech cannot perhaps be better described than in the terms in which my notes, made during the investigation, were afterwards summarized in my published report.[2] These

[1] "The Journal of American Folk-Lore" for July, 1888, p. 123.
[2] "United States Exploring Expedition, under Charles Wilkes,

will here be given with such additional information as later inquiries have procured.

The British and American trading ships first appeared on the north-west coast during the closing years of the last century. The great number of languages spoken by the native tribes proved to be a serious hindrance to their business. Had it chanced that any one of these languages was of easy acquisition and very generally diffused, like the Chippeway among the eastern tribes, the Malay in the Indian Archipelago, and the Italian in the Mediterranean, it would, no doubt, have been adopted as the medium of communication between the whites and the natives. Unfortunately, all these languages—the Nootka, Nisqually, Chinook, Chihailish, and others—were alike harsh in pronunciation, complex in structure, and each spoken over a very limited space. The foreigners, therefore, took no pains to become acquainted with any of them. But, as the harbour of Nootka was at that time he headquarters or chief emporium of the trade, it was necessarily the case that some words of the dialect there spoken became known to the traders, and that the Indians, on the other hand, were made familiar with a few English words. These, with the assistance of signs, were sufficient for the slight intercourse that was then maintained. Afterwards the traders began to frequent the Columbia River, and naturally attempted to communicate with the natives there by means of the words

U.S.N.," vol. vii., "Ethnography and Philology," by Horatio Hale, 1846, pp. 635-650.

which they had found intelligible at Nootka. The Chinooks, who are quick in catching sounds, soon acquired these words, both Nootka and English, and we find that they were in use among them as early as the visit of Lewis and Clark, in 1804.

But when, at a later period, the white traders of Astor's expeditions, and from other quarters, made permanent establishments in Oregon, it was soon found that the scanty list of nouns, verbs, and adjectives then in use was not sufficient for the more constant and general intercourse which began to take place. A real language, complete in all its parts, however limited in extent, was required; and it was formed by drawing upon the Chinook for such words as were requisite, in order to add to the skeleton which they already possessed the sinews and tendons, the connecting ligaments, as it were, of a speech. These consisted of the numerals (the ten digits and the word for hundred), twelve pronouns (I, thou, he, we, ye, they, this, other, all, both, who, what), and about twenty adverbs and prepositions (such as—now, then, formerly, soon, across, ashore, off-shore, inland, above, below, to, with, &c.). Having appropriated these and a few other words of the same tongue, the Trade Language —or, as it now began to be styled, "the Jargon"— assumed a regular shape, and became of great service as a means of general intercourse.

But the new idiom received additions from other sources. The Canadian *voyageurs*, as they are called, who enlisted in the service of the American and British fur companies, were brought more closely in contact with the Indians than any others of the foreigners. They did not merely trade, they travelled, hunted, ate, and, in short, lived with them on terms of familiarity. The consequence was, that several words of the French language were added to the slender stock of the Jargon. These were only such terms as did not previously belong to it, including the names of various articles of food and clothing in use among the Canadians (bread, flour, overcoat, hat), some implements and articles of furniture (axe, pipe, mill, table, box), several of the parts of the body (head, mouth, tongue, teeth, neck, hand, foot), and, characteristically enough, the verbs to run, sing, and dance. A single conjunction or connective particle, *puis*, corrupted to *pe*, and used with the various meanings of then, besides, and, or, and the like, was also derived from this source.

Eight or ten words were made by what grammarians term onomatopœia,—that is, were formed by a rude attempt to imitate sound, and are therefore the sole and original property of the Jargon. Considering its mode of formation, one is rather surprised that the number of these words is not greater. *Liplip* is intended to express the sound of boiling water, and means to boil. *Tingting*, or, more commonly, *tintin* (for the nasal sound is difficult to these Indians) is the ringing of a bell, and thence any instrument of music. *Po*, or *poo*, is the report of a gun; *tiktik* is for a watch; *tumtum* is the word for heart, and is intended to represent its beating. The word *tum*, pronounced with great force, dwelling on the concluding *m*, is the nearest approach which the natives can make to the noise of a cataract; but they usually join with it the English word *water*, making *tum-wata*, the name which they give to the falls of a river. *Mash* represents the sound of anything falling or thrown down (like the English *mash* and *smash*); *klak* is the sound of a rope suddenly loosed from its fastenings, or "let go."

All the words thus combined in this singularly constructed language, at that stage of its existence, were found to number, according to my computation, about two hundred and fifty. Of these, eighteen were of Nootka origin, forty-one were English, thirty-four French, one hundred and eleven Chinook, ten formed by onomatopœia, and some thirty-eight were of doubtful derivation, though probably for the most part either Chinook or Nootkan. But, as might be expected, the language continued to develop. Its grammar, such as it was, remained the same, but its lexicon drew contributions from all the various sources which have been named, and from some others. In 1863, seventeen years after my list was published, the Smithsonian Institution put forth a "Dictionary of the Chinook Jargon," prepared by the late George Gibbs, a thoroughly competent investigator. His collection comprised nearly five hundred words. Those of Chinook origin had almost doubled, being computed at two hundred and twenty-one. The French had more than doubled, and comprised now ninety-four words. The English terms were sixty-seven. The great Salish or "Flathead" stock, with whose tribes, next to the Chinook, the Oregon traders had the largest relations, furnished thirty-nine words. The Nootka, in its various dialects, now yielded twenty-four. The others, about forty, were due to the imitation of natural sounds, or were of casual or undetermined derivation.

The origin of some of the words is rather whimsical. The Americans, British, and French are distinguished by the terms *Boston*, *Kinchotsh* (King George), and *Pasaiuks*, which is presumed to be the word *Français* (as neither *f*, *r*, nor the nasal *n* can be pronounced by the Indians) with the Chinook plural termination *uks* added. The word for blanket, *paseesee*, is probably from the same source (*françaises*, French goods or clothing). "Foolish" is expressed by *pelton* or *pilton*, derived from the name of a deranged person, one Archibald Pelton, whom the Indians saw at Astoria; his strange appearance and actions made such an impression upon them, that thenceforward anyone behaving in an absurd or irrational manner, was said to act *kahkwa Pelton*, "like Pelton," but the word is now used without the preceding particle.

Since the publication of the vocabulary of Gibbs, no material change seems to have been made in the language. Two later dictionaries of the Jargon have come into my hands—small pamphlets, both printed in Victoria, B.C., the one in 1878, and the other as late as 1887. The former is announced as the "sixth edition," and the latter is described as a "new edition"—facts which

sufficiently prove the continued and extensive use of
this "international speech." There can be no doubt
that it will remain a living and useful language so long
as the native tribes continue to speak their own dialects.
Rude and almost formless as it is, the spontaneous pro-
duct of the commercial needs of mingled races, it has
been the source of great and varied benefits. It may
well serve, if not as a model, at least as a finger-post to
direct us to some higher invention for subserving the
larger uses of an advanced civilization. Viewed in this
light, and also as presenting one of the most curious
specimens of a "mixed language" which philologists
have had the opportunity of analyzing, the Jargon seems
to merit a somewhat careful study.

## Orthography and Pronunciation.

In my original account of this language, the usual
"scientific orthography" was adopted. The vowels had
their "continental" sounds (as in German or Italian),
and the consonants their English pronunciation. But
what was then a purely oral idiom has now become a
written language. Books have been printed in it, and
dictionaries published, in which the English orthography
has been adopted. The defects of this orthography are
well known, but, under the circumstances, we have no
choice but to follow it, making up for its deficiencies by
the necessary explanations.

In the phonetics of the language one point is specially

interesting, both as illustrating the usual result of the fusion of two or more languages, and as showing one of the laws which must govern the formation of any international speech. As the Jargon is to be spoken by Englishmen and Frenchmen, and by Indians of at least a dozen tribes, so as to be alike easy and intelligible to all, it must admit no sound which cannot be readily pronounced by all. The numerous harsh Indian gutturals either disappear entirely, or are softened to *h* and *k*.[1] On the other hand, the *d, f, q, r, v, z*, of the English and French become in the mouth of a Chinook *t, p, k, l, w*, and *s*. The English *j* (dzh) is changed to *ch* (tsh); the French nasal *n* is dropped, or is retained without its nasal sound. The following examples will serve to illustrate these and other changes. In writing the Indian words, the gutturals are expressed by *gh* (or *kh*) and *q*, and the vowels have their Italian sounds:

| Chinook. | Jargon. | Meaning. |
|---|---|---|
| *taqegh,* | *ikeh',* | to wish, will, desire. |
| *thliakso,* | *yakso,* | hair. |
| *eleghe,* | *illahee,* | earth, land, country. |
| *etsghot,* | *itshoot,* | bear. |
| *opthleke,* | *opitlkeh,* | bow. |
| *tkalaitanam,* | *kali'tan,* | arrow, shot, bullet. |
| *taghka,* | *yahka,* | he, his. |
| *ntshaika,* | *nesi'ka,* | we. |
| *mshaika,* | *mesi'ka,* | ye. |

[1] Some writers, however, retain in the Jargon the "digraph" *gh*, to express, in some words of Chinook origin, the sound of the German gutteral *ch* in *Buch*.

## ORTHOGRAPHY AND PRONUNCIATION.

| Chinook. | Jargon. | Meaning. |
|---|---|---|
| *thlaitshka,* | *klaska,* | they. |
| *ight,* | *ikt,* | one. |
| *tkhlon,* | *klone,* | three. |
| *kustoghtkin,* | *stotekin,* | eight. |

| English. | Jargon. | Meaning. |
|---|---|---|
| *handkerchief,* | *hak'atshum,* | handkerchief. |
| *cry,* | *cly, kali',* | cry, mourn. |
| *coffee,* | *kaupy,* | coffee. |
| *suppose,* | *spose, pos,* | if, supposing. |
| *stick,* | *stick,* | stick, wood, tree, wooden. |
| *fire,* | *piah,* | fire, cook, ripe. |
| *sun,* | *sun,* | sun, day. |
| *stone,* | *stone,* | stone, bone, anything solid. |
| *dry,* | *tly, dely',* | dry. |
| *warm,* | *waum,* | warm. |
| *cold,* | *kole, cole,* | cold, winter, year. |
| *skin,* | *skin,* | skin, bark. |

| French. | Jargon. | Meaning. |
|---|---|---|
| *courir,* | *kooley,* | run. |
| *la bouche,* | *laboos',* | mouth. |
| *la hache,* | *lahash',* | axe. |
| *la graisse,* | *lakles',* | grease. |
| *le mouton,* | *lemooto,* | sheep. |
| *le main,* | *lemah',* | hand. |
| *le loup,* | *leloo',* | wolf. |
| *poudre,* | *po'lalie,* | gunpowder. |
| *sauvage,* | *si'wash,* | Indian. |
| *chapeau,* | *seahpo,* | hat. |

As will be seen, the orthography of the Jargon is unsettled and capricious. Most writers spell Indian and French words "by the ear," but use the ordinary English spelling for the English words comprised in the language, without regard to uniformity.

## Grammar.

The grammatical rules are very simple. There are no inflections. The language has no article. The demonstrative pronoun, *okook*, this, occasionally supplies the place of the English *the*.

The genitive of nouns is determined merely by the construction; as, *kahta nem mika papa?* (lit., what name thy father), what is the name of your father?

The plural is in general not distinguished in speaking; sometimes *hyu*, many, is employed by way of emphasis.

The adjective precedes the noun, as in English and Chinook; as, *lasway hakatshum*, silk handkerchief; *mesahchie tilikum*, bad people.

Comparison is expressed by a periphrasis. "I am stronger than thou," would be *wake mika skookum kahkwa nika*, lit., "thou not strong as I." The superlative is indicated by adverbs; as, *hyas oleman okook canim*, that canoe is the oldest, lit., "very old that canoe;" *siah ahnkottie*, very ancient (lit., far ago). A great deal is expressed by the mere stress of the voice; *hyas″* (dwelling long on the last syllable) means exceedingly great. *Ahn″kottie*, with the first syllable drawn out, signifies very long ago; so *hyak″*, very quick; *hyu″*, a great many; *tenas″*, very small, &c.

The numerals are from the Chinook. They are—

# GRAMMAR.

*ikt*, one.
*moxt*, two.
*klone*, three.
*lakit*, four.
*kwinnum*, five.
*taghum*, or *tahkum*, six.

*sinamoxt*, seven.
*stotekin*, eight.
*kwaist*, nine.
*tahtlelum*, *tahtlum*, ten.
*takamonuk*, hundred.

The combinations of the numerals are the simplest possible. Eleven is *tahtlum pe ikt*, ten and one; twelve is *tahtlum pe moxt*, &c. Twenty is *moxt tahtlum;* thirty, *klone tahtlum*. Thousand is *tahtlum takamonuk*. "Eighteen hundred and eighty-nine" would be *tahtlum pe stotekin takamonuk stotekin tahtlum pe kwaist*.

The personal pronouns are—

*nika*, I.
*mika*, thou.
*yahka*, he.

*nesika*, we.
*mesika*, ye.
*klaska*, they.

*Nasaika* (or *ntshaika*) in Chinook means "we here," excluding the person addressed. In the Jargon, *nesika* is used in a more general sense, though *alhika* (in Chinook *alghaika*), which means "we all" (including the person addressed), is sometimes employed by those who understand the native idiom.

The personal pronouns become possessive merely by being prefixed to nouns; as, *nika house*, my house; *mika papa*, thy father; *nesika illahee*, our land.

The interrogative pronouns are, *klaksta*, who? *kata* or *ikta*, what? and *kunjik*, how many or how much? The latter is also used for when? *i.e.* how much time, how many days?

The relative pronouns must, in general, be understood; as, *kah okoke sahmun mika wawa nika?* where is that salmon [of which] you told me? Sometimes, however, the interrogative pronouns supply their place, as in English; thus, *wek nika kumtuks ikta mika wawa,* I do not understand what you say.

*Okoke,* this or that, is the only demonstrative pronoun.

The indefinite pronouns are, *kunamoxt,* both; *halo,* none; *konaway,* all; *hyu,* much or many; *tenas,* few or little; *huloima,* other.

In general, the tense of the verb is left to be inferred from the context. When it is absolutely necessary to distinguish the time, certain adverbs are employed; as, *chee,* just now, lately; *alta,* now, at present; *winapie,* presently; *alkie,* soon; *ahnkuttie,* formerly; *okoke-sun,* to-day; *tomolla,* to-morrow; *tahlkie,* yesterday.

The future, in the sense of "about to," "ready to," is sometimes expressed by *tikeh* or *tikegh,* which means properly to wish or desire; as, *nika papa tikegh mimaloose,* my father is near dying, or about to die.

A conditional or suppositive meaning is given to a sentence by the words *klonass,* perhaps, and *spose* (from the English "suppose") used rather indefinitely. *Nika kwass nika papa klonass mimaloose,* I fear my father will die (lit., I afraid my father perhaps die). *Spose mika klatawa yahwa, pe nika chaco kahkwa,* if you will go yonder, I will follow (lit., suppose you go that way, then I come the same). *Na* (or *nah*) is a common interrogative particle; *sick na mika,* are you sick?

The substantive verb is always to be understood from the form of the sentence; as, *mika pelton*, thou art foolish; *hyas oluman mika house*, very old (is) thy house.

The adverb usually precedes the adjective or verb which it qualifies, though it may sometimes follow the latter; as, *hyas kloshe*, very good; *nika hyas tikeh kumtuks*, I very much wish to know; *pahtlatch weght*, give more, or again.

There is but one true preposition, *kopa*, which is used in various senses,—to, for, at, in, among, about, towards, &c.; but even this may generally be omitted, and the sentence remain intelligible. *Nika klatawa nika house* (I go my house) can only mean "I am going to my house." *Keekwilie*, down, is used in the sense of "beneath," and *saghalie*, high up, in the sense of "above." *Kunamoxt*, both, or together, is sometimes used in the sense of "with."

Only two conjunctions, properly speaking, are found in the language—*pe*, from the French word *puis*, used to mean and, or, then, but, &c., and *spose* (often contracted to *pos*), from "suppose," employed in the sense of if, when, in case that, provided that, and in general, as has been said, as a sign of the subjunctive or conditional mood.

It will be noticed that these two conjunctions form the only exceptions to the rule that all the grammatical elements of the Jargon are derived from the proper Chinook language. The pronouns and the numerals are pure Chinook. The fact thus brought to view accords with the well-known law of linguistic science, that in every mixed language the grammar is mainly derived from one of the constituent idioms, which must consequently determine the stock of the composite speech. The Oregon Trade Language, though framed mainly by English-speaking men, must be held to be, philologically, a dialect of the Chinook stock, just as the English, in spite of its immense store of Romanic words, is properly classed as a Teutonic idiom.

It may not at first be easy to comprehend how a language composed of so few words, thus inartificially combined, can be extensively used as the sole medium of communication among many thousand individuals. Various circumstances, however, are to be borne in mind in estimating its value as such a medium. In the first place, it is to be observed that many of the words have a very general sense, and may receive different, though allied significations, according to the context. Thus *mahkook* is to trade, buy, sell, or barter, and, as a noun, a dealing, bargain, or exchange; *hyas mahkook* (great bargain) signifies dear or precious; *tenas mahkook* (small bargain), cheap. *Sahhalie* (or *saghalie*) expresses above, up, over, high, tall, and, as a noun, the upper region, heaven. *Stik*, or *stick*, is stick, wood, tree, forest, club, cane. *Solleks* is angry, hostile, to quarrel, fight. *Mitlite* is to sit, reside, remain, stop, and may also express to have and to be; as, *mitlite hyu sahmun kopa mika?* have you plenty of salmon? (lit., remains much salmon to you?) *Muckamuck* is to take anything into the mouth;

hence, *muckamuck sahmun*, to eat salmon; *muckamuck chuck*, to drink water; *muckamuck kinootl*, to smoke or chew tobacco.

But it is in the faculty of combining and compounding its simple vocables—a power which it doubtless derives, in some degree, from its connection with the Indian tongues—that the Jargon has its capacity for expression almost indefinitely extended. Three or four hundred words may be learned without difficulty in a week or two, and a very short time will make the learner familiar with their ordinary use and construction. He will then have no difficulty in understanding the numerous compounds which, if they had been simple words, would have cost him much additional labour. Almost every verb and adjective may receive a new signification by prefixing *mamook*, to make or cause. Thus, *mamook chaco* (to make to come), to bring; *mamook klatawa* (make to go), to send or drive away; *mamook po* (make blow), to fire a gun; *mamook kloshe* (make good), to repair, adorn, put in order, cure; *mamook keekwilee* (put low), to put down, lower, bury; *mamook klimmin* (make soft, or fine in substance), to soften, as a skin—also, to grind, as wheat; *mamook papeh* (make paper), to write or draw; *mamook kumtuks* (make to know), to teach.

The following instances will show the usual mode of forming compound terms. From the English words (adopted into the Jargon) *man, ship, stick, stone, sail, house, skin*, are formed *shipman*, sailor; *shipstick*, mast or spar; *stickskin*, bark; *sailhouse*, tent; *stickstone*, a piece of petrified wood. The latter term was used by a native who saw a geologist collecting specimens of that description; whether it was composed on the spot, or was already in use, is not known. *Hyu-house* (many houses) is the common term for town; *cole-illahee, waum-illahee* (cold country, warm country), mean summer and winter. *Cole-sick-waum-sick* (cold sickness, warm sickness), pronounced as one word, is the expressive term for the ague-fever. *Kopet kumtuks* (no longer know) means to forget. *Tenas-man* (little man) is the term for boy; *tenas klootshman* (little woman), for girl. The usual expression for God is *Saghalie-Tyee*, lit. above-chief, or the heavenly chief. *Tum*, heavy noise, and *wata*, make *tum-wata*, a cataract. *Cole-snass* (cold rain) is snow.

Finally, in the Jargon, as in the spoken Chinese, a good deal is expressed by the tone of voice, the look, and the gesture of the speaker. The Indians in general—contrary to what seems to be a common opinion—are very sparing of their gesticulations. No languages, probably, require less assistance from this source than theirs. Every circumstance and qualification of their thought are expressed in their speech with a minuteness which, to those accustomed only to the languages of Europe, appears exaggerated and idle,—as much so as the forms of the German and Latin may seem to the Chinese. We frequently had occasion to observe the sudden change produced when a party of natives, who had been conversing in their own tongue, were joined by a foreigner, with whom it was necessary to speak in the Jargon. The countenances which had before been grave, stolid, and inexpressive, were instantly lighted up with animation; the low, monotonous tone became lively and modulated; every feature was active; the head, the arms, and the whole body were in motion, and every look and gesture became instinct with meaning. One who knew merely the subject of the discourse might often have comprehended, from this source alone, the general purport of the conversation.

### The Past and Future of the Jargon.

The notes from which the foregoing account of the Trade Language has been chiefly drawn were made, shortly before the middle of the century, at Fort Vancouver, on the Columbia River, then the headquarters of the Hudson's Bay Company in Oregon. The following description, written at the time, may be cited, as possessing now some historical interest:—

"The place at which the Jargon is most in use is at Fort Vancouver. At this establishment five languages are spoken by about five hundred persons, namely, the English, the Canadian French, the Chinook, the Cree, and the Hawaiian. The three former are already accounted for. The Cree is the language spoken in the families of many officers and men belonging to the Hudson's Bay Company, who have married half-breed wives at the ports east of the Rocky Mountains. The Hawaiian is in use among about a hundred natives of the

Sandwich Islands, who are employed as labourers about the Fort. Besides these five languages, there are many others, the Chehalis, Wallawalla, Calapooya, Nisqually, &c., which are daily heard from the natives who visit the Fort for the purpose of trading. Among all these persons there are very few who understand more than two languages, and many who speak only their own. The general communication is, therefore, maintained chiefly by means of the Jargon, which may be said to be the prevailing idiom. There are Canadians and half-breeds who have married Chinook women, and can only converse with their wives in this speech; and it is the fact, strange as it may seem, that many young children are growing up to whom this factitious language is really the mother-tongue, and who speak it with more readiness and perfection than any other. Could the state of things which exists there be suffered to remain a century longer, the result might be the formation of a race and idiom whose affinities would be a puzzle to ethnographers. The tide of population, however, which is now turning in this direction, will soon overwhelm and absorb all these scattered fragments of peculiar lineage and speech, leaving no trace behind but such as may exist on the written page."

The concluding prediction, which seemed at the time well warranted, has been but partly fulfilled. The language, in fact, seems destined to a long life and wide usefulness, though in a region somewhat remote from its original seat. On the site of Fort Vancouver it is now only heard from stray Indians who have wandered thither from their reservations. But on the reservations and in the interior it is still in frequent use. Its great field of usefulness, however, is now, as has been said, in the northern regions. In British Columbia and in parts of Alaska it is the prevailing medium of intercourse between the whites and the natives. There, too, the Indian tribes are not likely to die out. Along the rugged coast and in the mountainous interior there are friths and defiles which the white settler disdains, but where the hardy native fishermen, hunters, and trappers find ample means of livelihood. These natives seem destined to be hereafter to the whites of the valleys and towns what the Lapps are to the Swedes, and the Samoyeds to the Russians, an alien race of semi-barbarous but peaceful borderers, maintaining their own customs and languages, but keeping up a friendly commerce with their civilized neighbours. This commerce will probably be carried on for centuries by means of the Trade Language. When we note the persistency with which such isolated tribes preserve their own idioms—as in Wales, in the Scottish Highlands, in the Pyrenees and the Caucasus— we may find reason to believe that the Jargon will still have its office of an international speech to fulfil, among the many-languaged tribes of North-Western America, for hundreds, and perhaps thousands, of years to come.

## The Language as Spoken.

In addition to the examples of construction given in the foregoing pages, the following colloquial phrases, written down as they were heard from the natives and others versed in the idiom, will show the manner in which it is employed as a medium of ordinary intercourse :—

| | |
|---|---|
| *Nah, siks!* | Ho! friend! |
| *K'lahowyah.* | Good day! (the common salutation). |
| *Kah mika house?* | Where is your house? |
| *Kah mika klatawa?* | Where are you going? |
| *Kah mika chahko?* | Whence come you? |
| *Pahtlatch chuck.* | Give me some water. |
| *Hyas olo chuck nika.* | I am very thirsty. |
| *Hyas olo muckamuck.* | Very hungry. |
| *Nika klatawa kopa canim.* | I am going in a canoe. |
| *Kopet wawa.* | Do not talk. |
| *Kunjik mika tillikum?* | How many are your people? |
| *Tahtlum pe klone house konaway.* | Thirteen houses in all. |
| *Nika tikeh muckamuck mowitsh.* | I want to eat some venison. |
| *Kunjik sahmun mika makook chahko?* | How many salmon do you bring to trade? |
| *Moxt tahtlum pe quinnum.* | Twenty-five. |
| *Kahta okok win?* | How was the wind? (What that wind?) |
| *Hyas win. Halo win.* | Strong wind. No wind. |
| *Okok sun hyas waum.* | The sun (or day) was very warm. |
| *Kahta nem mika papa?* | What is the name of your father? |
| *Sick mika papa?* | Is your father sick? |

## COLLOQUIAL AND NARRATIVE PHRASES. 23

| | |
|---|---|
| *Kokshut yahka lepee.* | His leg is broken. |
| *Nawitha hyas klahowyam yahka.* | Truly he is very miserable. |
| *Mika na kumtuks alkie snass?* | Do you think it will rain? |
| *Okook stick klatawa illahie.* | That tree fell to the ground. |
| *Nika hyas tikeh kumtuks mamook papeh.* | I wish very much to learn to write. |
| *Ahnkottie hyas nika kumtuks kapswalla; alta kelapi nika tumtum.* | Formerly I used to (lit. knew to) steal much; now my heart is changed. |
| *Iktah mika wake klatawa kokshut eena,—alke mika mahkook musket.* | Why do you not go and kill beaver,—and then buy a gun? |
| *Nawitka konaway nesika tillikum memaloose.* | Truly all our people are dead. |
| *Hyas kloshe okook moola; hyak okook mamook klimminklimmin okook sapolil.* | Very good is that mill; quickly it grinds (makes fine) the corn. |
| *Wake nesika kumtuks waykut; kopa illahie klatawa ship; kalo chuck; hyas win; kokshut; klimmin chahko; alta klatawa keekwilee chuck; wake klaksta memaloose; konaway klatawa mahtwillie.* | We did not know the channel; the ship went aground; there was no water (to float it); a strong wind; it perished; went to pieces; then sank down under water; nobody was drowned; all got ashore. |
| *Nesika solleks mesahchie tillikum; klone nesika kokshut; moxt kahkwa hyoo nesika.* | We fought the enemy (bad people); we killed three; they were twice as many as we. |

The language has already the beginning of a literature. It has its songs, mostly composed by women, who sing them to plaintive native tunes. One of these simple songs, with its music, is given by Mr. J. G. Swan in his volume, "The North-West Coast," published in 1855. It might be styled "Annawillee's Lament." The deserted wife thus reproves her faithless husband:

| | |
|---|---|
| *Kah mika klatawa?* | Where hast thou gone? |
| *Kah mika klatawa?* | Where hast thou gone? |
| *Konaway sun* | Every day |
| *Hyu kely* | Greatly mourns |
| *Annawillee.* | Annawillee. |
| | |
| *Oh, nika tenas!* | Oh, my little one! |
| *Hyas klahowyam!* | Very wretched! |
| *Hyu kely,* | Greatly mourns, |
| *Konaway sun,* | Every day, |
| *Nika tenas.* | My little one. |
| | |
| *Konaway halo* | All gone is |
| *Nesika muckamuck;* | Our food; |
| *Wake-siah mimaloose* | Soon will die |
| *Nika tenas.* | My little one. |

Dr. Franz Boas, during his recent visits to British Columbia, has collected many of these artless little effusions, which he has published in the "Journal of American Folk-lore" for December, 1888. Several of them have at least the poetry which a touch of true pathos will always give. Here are some that, as we are told, "refer to the parting of friends, and greetings to those staying at home":

| | |
|---|---|
| *Klonas kahta nika tumtum;* | I know not how my heart feels; |
| *Kwanesum nika tikeh nanitsh mika;* | Ever I wish to see you; |
| *Alkie nika wawa klahowya. Ya aya!* | Soon must I say farewell. Ah me! |
| | |
| *Hayaleha, hayaleha, hayaleha!* | Ah me! ah me! ah me! |
| *Spose mika nanitsh nika tillikum,* | When you see my people, |
| *Wake-siah nika mimaloose alta,* | (Say) Almost I am dead now, |
| *Kopa Koonspa illahie. Yaya!* | In Queensboroughland. Ah me! |

| | |
|---|---|
| *Yah! konaway sun nika sick tumtum,* | Ah! every day I am sick at heart, |
| *Kopa nika man kopa Kaliponia.* | For my husband in California. |

Then we have some of the rude "songs of love and jealousy" that float among the motley throngs of Indians and sailors in the native shanties which form the suburbs of Victoria, Vancouver, and New Westminster:

| | |
|---|---|
| *Klonas kahta nika tumtum* | I know not how my heart is |
| *Kopa Johnny.* | Toward Johnny. |
| *Okook tenas man mamook pelton nika.* | That young man makes a fool of me. |
| *Aya!* | Ah me! |
| *Yaya!* | Ah me! |
| *Spose mika iskum klotshman,* | If you take a wife, |
| *Yaya!* | Ah me! |
| *Wake mika solleks nika.* | Do not quarrel with me. |
| *Kultus kopa nika.* | It is nothing to me. |
| *Kultus kopa nika* | It is nothing to me |
| *Spose mika mahsh nika.* | If you desert me. |
| *Hyu tenas man koolie kopa town;* | Many young men go about town; |
| *Alkie wekt nika iskum.* | Soon again I take one. |
| *Wake kul kopa nika.* | That is not hard for me. |
| *Aya, aya!* | Ah me! ah me! |
| *Ellip nika nanitsh* | Soon shall I see |
| *Sitka, mesika illahie.* | Sitka, your country. |
| *Kultus spose nika mimaloose* | No matter if I die |
| *Yakwa ellip.* | There speedily. |

The missionaries, among whom, both in Oregon and in British Columbia, there have been men of more than ordinary talent and cultivation, have not failed to turn to account this fondness of the natives for verse and song.

The Rev. Myron Eells, missionary on the Skokomish Reservation, well known for his valuable contributions to ethnological science and religious literature, has prepared and published a little collection of "Hymns in the Chinook Jargon Language," in which the difficulty of expressing moral and religious truths in this limited and purely material speech has been overcome with much skill. The following is sung to the tune of "John Brown":

| | |
|---|---|
| *Jesus chaco kopa saghalie;* | Jesus came from heaven; |
| *Jesus hias kloshe.* | Jesus is very good. |
| *Jesus wawa kopa tillikums;* | Jesus taught the people; |
| *Jesus hias kloshe.* | Jesus is very good. |
| *Jesus wawa, wake kliminwhit;* | Jesus said, do not lie; |
| *Jesus hias kloshe.* | Jesus is very good. |
| *Jesus wawa, wake kapswalla;* | Jesus said, do not steal; |
| *Jesus hias kloshe.* | Jesus is very good. |
| *Kopa nika Jesus mimaloose;* | For me Jesus died; |
| *Jesus hias kloshe.* | Jesus is very good. |
| *Jesus klatawa kopa saghalie;* | Jesus went to heaven; |
| *Jesus hias kloshe.* | Jesus is very good. |
| *Alta Jesus mitlite kopa saghalie;* | Now Jesus lives in heaven; |
| *Jesus hias kloshe.* | Jesus is very good. |
| *Yahwa Jesus tikegh nika klatawa;* | There Jesus wishes me to go; |
| *Jesus hias kloshe.* | Jesus is very good. |

The following, entitled "Heaven," is sung to the tune of "Greenville." A literal version shows that the hymn is not devoid of poetical sentiment:

| | |
|---|---|
| *Kopa saghalie konoway tillikums*<br>  *Halo olo, halo sick;*<br>*Wake kliminwhit, halo sollecks,*<br>  *Halo pahtlum, halo cly.* | In high heaven all the people<br>  Do not hunger, are not sick;<br>Say no falsehood, never quarrel,<br>  Are not drunken, do not weep. |
| CHORUS—<br>*Jesus mitlite kopa saghalie,*<br>*Kunamoxt konoway tillikums kloshe.* | Jesus dwells in heaven above,<br>With all people who are good. |
| *Yahwa tillikums wake klahowya,*<br>  *Wake sick tumtum, halo till,*<br>*Halo mimaloose, wake mesachie,*<br>  *Wake polaklie, halo cole.* | There the people are not wretched,<br>  Not sad-hearted, never tired;<br>There they die not, are not wicked,<br>  There no darkness is, no cold. |
| *Yahwa tillikums mitlite kwanesum,*<br>  *Hiyu houses, hiyu sing;*<br>*Papa, mama, pe kloshe tenas,*<br>  *Wakut yaka chikamin pil.* | There the people dwell for ever,<br>  Many a home there, many a hymn;<br>Father, mother, and good children,<br>  In the streets of yellow gold. |
| *Jesus potlatch kopa siwash,*<br>  *Spose mesika hias kloshe,*<br>*Konoway iktas mesika tikegh,*<br>  *Kopa saghalie kwanesum.* | Jesus will bestow on Indians,<br>  If you all are very good,<br>All the things that you can long for,<br>  In high heaven evermore. |

Mr. Eells has been accustomed for many years to preach to the Indians in the Jargon, and he mentions the curious fact that he sometimes even thinks in this idiom. I am indebted to his kindness for the copy of a sermon which was preached in August, 1888, and which he has been good enough to put in manuscript for me.

It will serve to show how this language, limited as it is in vocabulary, can be made a vehicle, not merely of instruction, but also of effective argument and persuasion. Before giving the original, with its interlinear translation, it may be well to prefix a version in ordinary English, in which form, as will be seen, it becomes such a discourse as might have been addressed to the white pupils of a Sunday school in England or America. Mr. Eells writes: "By way of explaining it, I ought to say that, in speaking to the Indians, I am accustomed to use some large pictures, which I refer to; also that on the previous Sabbath I had been at Walla Walla, celebrating the semi-centennial of the organization of the first Presbyterian church in this region."

MATT. xxviii. 18, 19.

"Two Sundays ago I spoke to you concerning that picture. There you saw two women coming to the sepulchre where Jesus lay, on Sunday, just at sunrise. When they came to the sepulchre they did not see Jesus. Jesus had risen; He was gone. So I told you in that sermon.

"To-day I wish to explain to you about this picture. After Jesus had risen, He continued on the earth forty days. When the forty days were ended, He desired to ascend to heaven. So He led the people out of the city to that place where you behold them. Here you see Jesus. There are those people. Jesus wished to give good instructions to the people before He returned to heaven.

"Now I will explain to you the teaching of Jesus to those people. He said to them: 'It is good that you should go to every country in all the world, and carry the Gospel to all nations.' Thus spoke Jesus to them.

"Jesus was aware that all the nations of the world had no knowledge of the Gospel. They knew nothing of the happy home in heaven. They knew nothing of the Devil's home in the great fire. Jesus knew that the soul of a man is truly precious; that it is more precious than all the money and everything else in the world. So He wished His people, His missionaries, to go everywhere, and to help all people to leave the Devil's way, and to find the way of Jesus.

"They accepted the teaching of Jesus. One man went to one country; another man went to another country; and others went to other lands. Thus it was with all these missionaries in ancient times. Jesus was gracious to them and to their work. Jesus helped them; and many people in many lands became Christians. Before all those early missionaries were dead, five hundred thousand people had become Christians.

"Now Jesus wishes us to do likewise. He wants us to help other people to become Christians. Perhaps He may wish us to go to a distant land, and tell the far-off people about Jesus' word. Perhaps not. Perhaps He may want us to speak to the people who are near at hand. Perhaps He wishes us to give some money to help the missionaries in those far-off lands. In distant lands—in China, in Africa—there are many heathens. They do not want missionaries in their countries; so they will give no money to missionaries in their countries. Where shall the missionaries get food and other things? It is good for us to give some money, and to send the money to the far-off missionaries, and help them to carry the words of Jesus to the distant nations. If we are poor and have not much money, we should give a little money. Such is the teaching of Jesus.

"Perhaps we really have no money. Then we should pray to God that He will help those far-off missionaries. Jesus will accept our prayers. Thus we shall help to carry the teaching of Jesus to all countries everywhere.

"You know that last Sunday I was not with you. I was far away, at a place called Walla Walla. And why did I go? Fifty years ago American missionaries came from a distant land to Walla Walla. They wished to tell the Indians of the Gospel of Jesus. Just fifty years ago they founded a church there. So now the Christian people desired to have a celebration. Fifty years ago these missionaries left their homes in their far American land, and did just as Jesus had taught. Nearly ten years they remained at Walla Walla. Then some bad Indians became very hostile to one missionary, named Dr. Whitman, and they killed him and his wife and other persons. Other missionaries became afraid of those Indians, and left that region. Perhaps many persons said, 'The teaching of Jesus was not good, when He said to the missionaries long ago, that they should go into all lands, and carry the Gospel to every people.'

"Was what they said right? No! Before Dr. Whitman died he had given good teaching to the Indians. Other missionaries had done the same. That teaching was like good seed. Now this has grown mightily. When I now go to Walla Walla, I see there an Indian missionary; he is of the Nez-percés nation. And I know that not far from Walla Walla there are now ten Indian missionaries and seven hundred Christians. Fifty years ago missionaries did according to the word of Jesus, and bore the Gospel to the Indians, like good seed; and now it has become great. Thus we know that the teaching of Jesus is very good teaching. Jesus wishes you to do the same. It is good that you should help other people to become Christians."

The following is the sermon in its original language, with an interlinear translation. A careful enumeration shows that to express the whole of its historic and descriptive details, its arguments and its appeals, only ninety-seven different words of the Jargon are required, and not a single grammatical inflection. We may learn from this striking evidence, as Mr. Eells suggests, with how slender a vocabulary and how little grammar a language can "get along." Of these ninety-seven words we find that forty-six are of Chinook origin, seventeen of Nootka, and two of Salish; twenty-three are English, seven are French, and two only are the special property of the Jargon.

Moxt Sunday ahnkuttie nika mamook kumtux mesika
*Two Sundays ago I made know you*
kopa okoke papeh. Yahwa mesika nanitch moxt
*about this paper (picture). There you saw two*
klootchmen. Klaska chaco kopa mimoloose-illahee, kah
*women. They came to death-place, where*
Jesus mitlite, kopa Sunday, kopa delate tenas sun.
*Jesus lay, on Sunday at just little (early) day.*
Spose klaska klap okoke mimaloose-illahee, klaska halo
*When they reached that death-place, they did not*
nanitch Jesus. Jesus get-up; yaka klatawa. Kahkwa
*see Jesus. Jesus had risen; he was gone. So*
nika wawa kopa mesika talkie Sunday.
*I spoke to you (in) discourse of Sunday (sermon).*
Okoke sun nika tikegh wawa kopa mesika kopa okoke
*This day I will speak to you about this*
papeh. Kimtah Jesus yaka get-up, yaka mitlite kopa
*picture. After Jesus he had risen, he continued on*
illahee lakit tahtlum sun. Spose kopet lakit tahtlum sun,
*earth four ten days. When ended four ten days,*
Jesus yaka tikegh klatawa kopa Saghalie. Kahkwa yaka
*Jesus he would go to Heaven. So he*
lolo yaka tillikums klahanie kopa town, kopa okoke illahie
*led those people out of town, to that place*
kah mesika nanitch klaska. Yahwa mesika nanitch Jesus.
*where you see them. There you see Jesus.*
Yahwa yaka tillikums. Jesus yaka tikegh potlatch kloshe
*There those people. Jesus he would give good*
wawa kopa yaka tillikums, elip yaka killapi kopa
*speech to those people before he returned to*
Saghalie.
*Heaven.*
Alta nika mamook kumtux mesika kopa Jesus yaka wawa
*Now I make know you about Jesus his speech*
kopa yaka tillikums. Yaka wawa kopa klaska : " Kloshe
*to those people. He said to them: " Good*

## A SERMON.

mesika klatawa kopa konoway illahee, konoway kah, pe
*you go to every country, every where, and*
lolo Bible wawa kopa konoway tillikums." Kahkwa Jesus
*carry Bible words to all nations."  So Jesus*
yaka wawa kopa klaska.
*he spoke to them.*

Jesus yaka kumtux konoway tillikums, konoway kah,
*Jesus he knew all nations, every where,*
halo kumtux kopa kloshe home kopa Saghalie. Klaska
*did not know about good home in Heaven. They*
halo kumtux kopa Lejaub yaka home kopa hias piah.
*did not know about the Devil his home in great fire.*
Jesus yaka kumtux ikt man yaka tumtum delate hias
*Jesus he knew a man his soul truly (of) great*
mahkook ; yaka elip hias mahkook kopa konoway dolla pe
*price; it more precious than all money and*
konoway iktas kopa konoway illahee. Kahkwa yaka
*all things in every country. So he*
tikegh yaka tillikums, yaka leplet, klatawa konoway
*wished those people, those missionaries, go every*
kah, pe help konoway tillikums mash Lejaub yaka
*where, and help all nations reject Satan his*
owakut, pe klap Jesus yaka owakut.
*way, and take Jesus his way.*

Klaska iskum Jesus yaka wawa. Ikt man klatawa kopa
*They received Jesus his words. One man went to*
ikt illahee ; huloima man klatawa kopa huloima illahee ;
*one country; another man went to another country;*
huloima man klatawa kopa huloima illahee ; kahkwa kopa
*another man went to another country; so with*
konoway okoke leplet ahnkuttie. Jesus chaco hias
*all those missionaries formerly. Jesus became very*
kloshe tumtum kopa klaska, kopa klaska mamook. Jesus
*good (in) heart to them, to their work. Jesus*
yaka help klaska ; pe hiyu tillikums kopa hiyu illahee
*he helped them; and many people in many countries*

D

klaska chaco Christian. Elip kopa konoway okoke
*they became Christians. Before that all those*
leplet mimaloose ahnkuttie, kwinnum tukamonuk thou-
*missionaries died anciently, five hundred thou-*
sand tillikums chaco Christian.
*sand persons became Christians.*
Alta Jesus tikegh nesika mamook kahkwa. Yaka tikegh
*Now Jesus wishes us to do likewise. He wishes*
nesika help huloima tillikums chaco Christian. Klonas
*us to help other people become Christians. Perhaps*
yaka tikegh nesika klatawa kopa siyah illahee, pe mamook
*he wishes us to go to far countries, and make*
kumtux siyah tillikums kopa Jesus yaka wawa. Klonas
*know far nations about Jesus his words. Perhaps*
halo. Klonas Jesus yaka tikegh nesika wawa kopa tillikums
*not. Perhaps Jesus he wishes us speak to people*
wake siyah. Klonas yaka tikegh nesika potlatch tenas
*not far-off. Perhaps he wishes us to give a little*
dolla, kahkwa nesika mamook help leplet kopa siyah
*money, so we make help missionaries in far*
illahee. Kopa siyah illahee, kopa China illahee, kopa
*countries. In far countries, in China country, in*
nigga yaka illahee, hiyu mesachie man mitlite. Klaska
*negro his country, many bad men live. They*
halo tikegh leplet kopa klaska illahee; kahkwa
*do not want missionaries in their countries; so*
klaska halo pay dolla kopa leplet kopa klaska
*they do not pay money to missionaries in their*
illahee. Kah okoke leplet iskum muckamuck pe
*countries. Where those missionaries get food and*
huloima iktas? Kloshe nesika potlatch tenas dolla, pe
*other things? Good we give little money, and*
nesika mash okoke dolla kopa siyah leplet, pe
*we send that money to distant missionaries, and*
mamook help klaska lolo Jesus yaka wawa kopa siyah
*make help them carry Jesus his words to distant*

## A SERMON.

tillikums. Spose nesika klahowya kopa dolla, pe halo
*nations. If we are poor in money, if not*
mitlite hiyu dolla, kloshe nesika potlatch tenas dolla.
*have much money, good we give little money.*
Kahkwa Jesus yaka wawa.
*So Jesus he said.*
Klonas nesika delate mitlite halo dolla. Spose kahkwa,
*Perhaps we really have no money. If so,*
kloshe nesika pray kopa Saghalie Tyee kloshe yaka help
*good we pray to Heavenly Chief kindly he help*
okoke siyah leplet. Spose nesika mamook kahkwa,
*those distant missionaries. If we do thus,*
Jesus yaka iskum nesika wawa. Kahkwa nesika help kopa
*Jesus he receives our words. So we help in*
lolo Jesus yaka wawa kopa konoway illahee konoway
*carrying Jesus his words to every nation every*
kah.
*where.*
    Mesika kumtux kopa talkie Sunday nika halo mitlite
*You know on sermon Sunday I did not stay*
kunamoxt mesika. Nika mitlite siyah kopa ikt illahee yaka
*with you. I stayed far-off in a place its*
nem Walla Walla. Pe kahta nika klatawa? Alta nika
*name Walla Walla. And why (did) I go? Now I*
mamook kumtux mesika. Kwinnum tahtlum cole ahnkuttie,
*make know you. Five ten winters ago,*
Boston leplet chaco kopa siyah illahee, kopa Walla
*American missionaries came to far country, to Walla*
Walla illahee. Klaska tikegh mamook teach siwash kopa
*Walla country. They would make teach Indian about*
Jesus yaka wawa. Delate kwinnum tahtlum cole ahnkuttie
*Jesus his words. Just five ten winters ago*
klaska mamook church yahwa. Kahkwa alta Christian
*they made church there. So now Christian*
tillikums tikegh chee mamook kloshe time. Kwinnum
*people wish just make good time. Five*

## THE OREGON TRADE LANGUAGE.

tahtlum cole ahnkuttie okoke leplet mash klaska
*ten winters ago those missionaries left their*
home kopa siyah Boston illahee, pe mamook delate
*home in far-off American land, and did just*
kahkwa Jesus yaka wawa. Wake siyah tahtlum cole
*as Jesus he said. Not far (nearly) ten winters*
klaska mitlite kopa Walla Walla illahee ; pe mesachie
*they stayed at Walla Walla country; but bad*
siwash chaco hias solleks kopa ikt leplet, Dr.
*Indians became very angry against one missionary, Dr.*
Whitman yaka nem, pe klaska mamook mimoloose yaka
*Whitman his name, and they made dead him*
pe yaka klootchman pe huloima tillikums. Huloima
*and his wife and other persons. Other*
leplet chaco kwass kopa siwash, pe mash siwash yaka
*missionaries became afraid of Indians, and left Indians their*
illahee. Klonas hiyu tillikums wawa, "Jesus yaka wawa
*country. Perhaps many persons said, "Jesus his words*
hias cultus, spose yaka wawa ahnkuttie kopa leplet,
*very foolish, when he said formerly to missionaries,*
kloshe klatawa kopa konoway illahee konoway kah, pe
*good go to every country every where, and*
lolo Bible kopa konoway tillikums." Okoke delate
*carry Bible to every nation." (Was) That true*
wawa? Halo. Elip okoke man, Dr. Whitman, yaka
*speech? No. Before that man, Dr. Whitman, he*
mimaloose, yaka potlatch kloshe wawa kopa siwash ;
*died, he gave good speech to Indians;*
huloima leplet mamook kahkwa. Okoke wawa
*other missionaries did likewise. That speaking*
kahkwa kloshe seed. Alta yaka chaco hias. Spose nika
*like good seed. Now this becomes great. When I*
chee klatawa kopa Walla Walla, nika nanitch yahwa ikt
*now go to Walla Walla, I see there an*
siwash leplet, Nez-Percé yaka illahee. Pe nika
*Indian missionary, Nez-Percés his country. And I*

## THE LORD'S PRAYER.

kumtux wake siyah kopa Walla Walla mitlite alta tahtlum
*know not far (near) to Walla Walla reside now ten*
siwash leplet, pe taghum tukamonuk Christian.
*Indian missionaries and six hundred Christians.*
Kwinnum tahtlum cole ahnkuttie, leplet mamook
*Five ten winters ago, missionaries did*
kahkwa Jesus yaka wawa, pe lolo Bible kopa siwash,
*as Jesus he said, and carried Bible to Indians,*
kahkwa kloshe seed, pe alta yaka chaco hias. Kahkwa
*like good seed, and now this becomes great. So*
nesika kumtux Jesus yaka wawa hias kloshe wawa. Jesus
*we know Jesus his speech very good speech. Jesus*
yaka tikegh mesika mamook kahkwa. Kloshe mesika
*he wishes you to do likewise. Good (that) you*
help huloima tillikums chaco Christian.
*help other people become Christians.*

To the foregoing may be added the version (showing at once the strength and the defects of this idiom) which Mr. Eells has given, in his Hymn-book, of

### THE LORD'S PRAYER.

Nesika Papa klaksta mitlite kopa Saghalie, kloshe
*Our Father who livest in the Above, good*
mika nem kopa konoway kah. Kloshe spose mika chaco
*thy name over everywhere. Good if thou become*
delate Tyee kopa konoway tillikums. Kloshe spose mika
*true Chief over all people. Good if thy*
tumtum mitlite kopa illahee kahkwa kopa Saghalie. Potlatch
*mind is on earth as in the Above. Give*
kopa nesika kopa okoke sun nesika muckamuck. Mamook
*to us during this day our food. Pi-*
klahowya nesika kopa nesika mesachie mamook, kahkwa
*ty us for our evil doing, as*

nesika mamook klahowya klaksta man spose yaka mamook
*we    do    pity    any    man    if    he    does*
mesachie kopa nesika. Wake mika lolo nesika kopa kah
*evil    to    us.    Not thou carry us    to where*
mesachie mitlite; pe spose mesachie klap nesika, kloshe
*evil    is;    but    if    evil    find    us,    good*
mika help nesika tolo okoke mesachie. Delate konoway
*thou help    us    conquer that    evil.    Truly    all*
illahee mika illahee, pe mika hias skokum, pe mika delate
*earth    thy    earth, and thou very strong, and thou truly*
hias kloshe; kahkwa nesika tikegh konoway okoke. Kloshe
*very good;    so    we    wish    all    this.    Good*
kahkwa.
*so.*

# TRADE LANGUAGE AND ENGLISH DICTIONARY.

IN writing the Jargon, philologists like George Gibbs and missionaries like Mr. Eells have been compelled, by the demands of the population for whom they wrote, to adopt the English orthography, with all its notorious imperfections. The result is, that in many cases it is impossible for a stranger to judge from the spelling of a word how it should be pronounced. Whether the *ow* in *klahowyah* is pronounced as in the English "how," or as in "know;" whether *nanitch* is sounded "nah-nitsh," or "nay-nitch;" whether *ahnkuttie* is accented on the first or on the second syllable, cannot be known from the orthography. In the dictionary, therefore, wherever any doubt can arise, the correct pronunciation is indicated in brackets, by employing the vowels with their Italian (or German) sounds: *a* as in father; *e* like *a* in fate; *i* as in machine; *ō* (long) as in note, or short (*ŏ*) as in not; *ū* like *oo* in pool, or short (*ŭ*) as in but; *ai* like *i* in pine; *au* like *ou* in loud. The acute accent (as in *klonás*) marks the syllable on which the stress of voice is placed. In many cases there are various spellings and different pronunciations, which are given as far as such minute accuracy has seemed likely to be useful.

The letters C., E., F., N., and S., refer to the derivation of words, and signify Chinook, English, French, Nootka, and Salish. Words marked J. are considered to be the peculiar property of the Jargon, as having been formed either in imitation of sounds or by some casual invention. Unmarked words are of doubtful origin.

In words derived from the Chinook language, the guttural sound represented by *ch* in German, and in old English by *gh*, is sometimes retained in the Jargon, and is expressed by *gh*, as in *saghalie, tikegh, weght*, and a few others. Speakers not familiar with this sound will be understood if they utter it as a strongly aspirated English *h*.

This dictionary, it should be stated, is, in the main, a copy (with some additions and corrections) of that of George Gibbs, published by the Smithsonian Institution in 1863, and now regarded as the standard authority, so far as any can be said to exist; but it may be added that the principal part of that collection was avowedly derived by the estimable compiler from my own vocabulary, published seventeen years before.

## A.

**Abba**, well then.
**Ahha**, C. [āha], yes. See *Eyeh*.
**Ahnkuttie, ahnkottie**, C. [ánkati, ánkoti], formerly, anciently, ago. *Moxt sun ahnkuttie*, two days ago.
**Alah**, J. [alá], ah! oh! Exclamation of surprise.
**Alip**, first, before. See *Elip*.
**Alkie**, C. [álke, álki], soon, presently, by-and-by.
**Alloima**. See *Huloima*.
**Alta**, C., now.
**Amota**, C. [amote], strawberry.
**Anah**, J. [aná], exclamation of pain or displeasure, ah! oh! fie!
**Appola**, anything roasted. See *Lapellah*.
**Ats**, C., younger sister.
**Ayahwhul**, S. [ayáhwŭl], to lend; to borrow.

## B.

**Bebee**, F. [bibi], to kiss, a kiss.
**Bed**, E., a bed.
**Bit**, E., a sixpenny piece; a dime.

**Bloom**, E., broom. *Mamook bloom*, to sweep.
**Boat**, E., boat.
**Boston**, American. *Boston illahee*, the United States.
**By-by**, E., by-and-by.

## C.

**Calipeen, calipee**, F., a rifle. (Fr. *carabine*.)
**Canim**, C. [kaním, kaném], canoe.
**Capo**, F. [kapó], coat.
**Chaco, chahko**, N. [cháko], to come; to become. *Chako kloshe*, to get well.
**Chakchak**, C., the bald eagle.
**Chee**, C., lately, just now; new.
**Chetlo**, S., oyster.
**Chetwoot**, S., black bear.
**Chikamin**, N. [chíkamin], iron, metal; metallic. *T'kope chikamin* (white metal), silver. *Pil chikamin*, or *chikamin pil* (yellow metal), gold, or copper.
**Chikchik**, J., waggon, cart, wheel.
**Chilchil**, C., button, star.
**Chitsh**, S., grandfather.

# DICTIONARY. 41

**Chope**, S., grandmother.
**Chotub**, S., flea.
**Chuck**, N., water, river. *Salt chuck*, the sea. *Skookum chuck* (powerful water), rapids.
**Chukkin**, S., to kick.
**Cly**, or **kely**, E. [kŭlaí], to cry, lament; mourning, weeping.
**Cole**, E., cold, winter, year. *Cole illahie* (cold country), winter. *Tahtlum cole*, ten years. *Kole-sick-waum-sick*, the ague-fever.
**Comb**, E., comb. *Mamook comb*, to comb. *Mamook comb illahie* (to comb the ground), to harrow.
**Cooley**, F. (*courir*), to run, go about.
**Coopcoop**, C., small dentalium, or shell money.
**Cosho**, F. (*cochon*), hog, pork. *Siwash cosho* (Indian pig), a seal.
**Cultus**, C., worthless, purposeless; merely, simply; nothing. *Cultus man*, worthless fellow. *Cultus potlatch*, free gift. *Cultus heehee*, a joke (merely laughter). *Cultus mitlite*, to sit idle (merely sitting).

### D.

**Delate**, **delett**, F. (*droite*) [delét], straight, direct, true; truly, exactly. *Delate kwinnum cole ahnkuttie*, just five years ago.

**Diaub**, or **yaub** (*diable*), devil. See *Lejaub*.
**Dly**, **dely**, E. [dŭlaí], dry.
**Doctin**, E., doctor.
**Dolla**, **tahla**, E. [tála], dollar; money. *Dolla seahost* (silver eyes), spectacles.

### E.

**Eyeh**, N. [iyéh], yes.
**Ehkahnam**, C. [ekánam], tale, story.
**Ehkoli**, C. [ekoli], whale.
**Eena**, C., beaver. *Eena stik* (beaver wood), willow.
**Eenapoo**, C. [ínapu], louse. *Sopen eenapoo* (jump-louse), flea.
**Ekkeh**, brother-in-law.
**Elahan**, **elann**, S. [ílahan, ilán], aid, alms. *Mamook elann*, to help.
**Elip**, or **ellip**, S. [ílip, or élip], first, before, sooner, more; soon, speedily. *Elip yaka mimoluse*, before he died. *Elip hias mahkook*, more precious.
**Elita**, C. [ilaíte], slave.
**Enati**, C., across, on the other side. See *Inati*.
**Esalth**, **yesalth** [isálth], Indian corn, maize.
**Ethlon**, C., fathom. See *Itlan*.

### G.

**Get-up**, or **ket-op**, E., to get up, rise; risen.

**Glease**, E., grease, fat, oil. *Glease piah*, candle. See *Lakless*.

## H.

**Hahlakl**, C., wide, open. *Mamook hahlakl la pote*, open the door.

**Hahthaht**, S., the mallard duck.

**Hakatshum**, E., handkerchief.

**Halo**, not, none, absent. *Halo mitlite* (nothing remains), empty. *Halo seahost* (no eyes), blind. *Halo ikta* (no goods), poor. *Halo dolla*, without money.

**Haul**, E., to haul, pull.

**Heehee**, J., to laugh, laughter, amusement. *Mamook heehee*, to make fun, to jest. *Heehee house*, place of amusement, as a tavern or bowling alley. *Heehee limah*, gambling.

**Help**, E., to help.

**Hias**, great. See *Hyas*.

**Hiyu**, much. See *Hyu*.

**Hohhoh**, J., to cough.

**Hokumelh**, S., to gather, glean.

**Home**, E., home.

**Hoolhool**, C., mouse. *Hyas hoolhool* (big mouse), rat.

**House**, E., house. *Mahkook house* (trading house), shop.

**Howh**, J. [hau], interj., yohoe! hurry! *Howh, howh, hurra!* Ho! ho! hurry up!

**Howkwutl**, C. [háukwŭtl], how could, cannot. *Howkwutl nika klatawa?* how could I go?

**Hullel**, C. [hullél], to shake.

**Huloima**, C., other, another, different.

**Humm**, J., bad odour; stinking. *Humm oputsh* (stinking tail), skunk.

**Hunlkih**, C., crooked, knotted, curled.

**Huyhuy**, J. [húihúi], bargain, exchange, barter; to change. *Huyhuy lasell*, change the saddle. *Huyhuy tumtum*, to change the mind.

**Hwah, hwahwa.** J. (exclamation of surprise, admiration, or earnestness), aha! dear me!

**Hyak**, C. [haíak], swift, quick; hurry! hasten!

**Hyas, hias**, N. [haiás], great; very. *Hyas tyee*, great chief. *Hias mahcook*, great price, dear. *Hyas ahnkottie*, long ago.

**Hykwa, hyakwa**, N., shell-money; the dentalium. See *Coopcoop*.

**Hyu, hyoo**, N. [haiú], much, many, plenty, enough. *Hyu tillikum*, many people. *Tenas hyu* (little many), some.

## I.

**Ikkik**, C., fishhook.
**Ikpooie**, C. [ikpúi], to shut, close ; closed, shut up. *Ikpooie lapote*, shut the door. *Ikpooie kwolann* (closed ear), deaf.
**Ikt**, C., one, once ; a, an. *Ikt man*, a man. *Ikt-ikt man*, someone or other. *Ikt nika klatawa kopa yaka house*, I went once to his house.
**Iktah**, ikta, C., what, why (same as *kahta*). *Iktah okook*, what is that?
**Iktah**, iktas, C., thing, goods. *Hyu tenas iktas*, many little things.
**Illahee**, illahie, C. [ílahi], the earth, land, dirt. *Saghalie illahee*, high land, mountain, heaven.
**Inati**, eenati, C. [ínatai], across, opposite. *Inati chuck*, on the other side of the river.
**Ipsoot**, C. [ípsut], to hide, keep secret ; hidden ; secretly.
**Isik**, C. [ísik], a paddle. *Mamook isik*, to paddle. *Isik stick* (paddle-wood), the elm.
**Iskum**, C., to take, receive, get, hold.
**Itlan**, it'hlan, C., a fathom ; the length of the extended arms.
**Itlokum**, C. [ítlokum], the game of "hand," a gambling game.
**Itlwillie**, ilwillie, C. [ítlwili], flesh, meat.
**Itswoot**, itshoot, C., the black bear. *Itshoot paseesie*, thick dark cloth or blankets.

## K.

**Kah**, C., where, whither, whence. *Kah mika mitlite*, where do you live? *Konoway kah*, everywhere.
**Kahdena**, C., to fight.
**Kahkah**, J., a crow.
**Kahkwa**, N., like, equal with, so, as, thus. *Kahkwa nika tumtum* (such my heart), so I think. *Kloshe kahkwa* (good so), that is right.
**Kahnaway**, C. [kánawe], acorns.
**Kahp'ho**, C., elder brother, sister, or cousin.
**Kahta**, C., how, why, what. *Kahta mika chaco?* why have you come? *Kata mika nem?* what is your name?
**Kalakalahma**, C., a goose.
**Kalakwahtie**, C. [kalakwáti], inner bark of the cedar ; woman's petticoat of bark. *Kalakwahtie stick*, cedar tree.
**Kalitan**, C. [kalaítan], arrow, bullet, shot. *Kalitan lesac*, quiver, shot-pouch.
**Kalakala**, kullakulla, C. [kalákala], bird, fowl.

**Kamass, camass, lakamass,** N., camass root, *Scilla esculenta.*
**Kamooks,** C. [kámuks], dog. *Kahkwa kamooks,* like a dog, beastly.
**Kamosuk,** C. [kamósŭk], beads.
**Kapsualla, kapswalla,** to steal.
**Katsuk, kotsuk,** C., middle, centre.
**Kaupy,** E., coffee.
**Kawak,** S. [kawák], to fly.
**Kawkawak,** C. [kákawak], yellow, or pale green.
**Keekwilee, keekwillie,** C. [kíkwili], low, below, under, down. *Mamook keekwilee,* to lower.
**Keepwot,** or **keepwah,** C., needle, thorn, sting of an insect. *Shoes keepwot,* an awl.
**Kehwa,** because.
**Kelapi, kilapie** [kílapai], to turn, return, overturn, upset. *Elip yaka kelapi,* before he returns. *Kelapi canem,* to upset a canoe. *Mamook kelapi,* to send back.
**Kely.** See *Cly.*
**Ketling,** or **kitling,** E., kettle, can, basin.
**Ket-op.** See *Get-up.*
**Keuatan,** C. [kíuatan], horse.
**Kilitsut,** C., flint, bottle, glass.
**Killapie.** See *Kelapi.*

**Kimta,** C., behind, after, afterwards, last, since.
**Kintshautsh,** E. [King George], English. *Kintshautsh man,* Englishman.
**Kinootl, kinoos,** C. [kaínutl], tobacco.
**Kishkish,** C., to drive, as cattle.
**Kiwa,** J. [kaíwa], crooked.
**Kiyah,** S., entrails.
**Klah,** C., free, clear; in sight.
**Klahanie,** C. [klahaní], out, without. *K'lahanie kopa town,* out of town.
**Klahowya,** C. [klahaúya], how do you do? good-bye! The common salutation.
**Klahowyam, klahowya,** C. [klahaúyăm], poor, wretched, pitiable, pitiful. *Mamook klahowyam,* to be pitiful or generous.
**Klahwa,** C., slow, slowly.
**Klak,** C., off, out, away. *Mamook klak,* take off, untie, put away.
**Klaksta,** C., who? what one? *Halo klaksta,* no one.
**Klakwan,** S., to wipe or lick.
**Klale,** C. [klēl], black, dark blue, or green; dark, ignorant.
**Klap,** C., to find.
**Klapite,** or **klapote,** C. [klépait], thread, twine.
**Klaseess,** C., stars.

**Klaska,** or **kluska,** C., they, their, them.
**Klatawa,** N., to go, walk.
**Klawhap,** C. [klahwáp], a hole.
**Klemahun,** S. [klémahŭn], to stab, wound, spear.
**Klementikote,** C., to lie. See *Kliminwhit.*
**Klitl,** or **klilt,** C., sour, bitter.
**Klikamuks,** C., blackberries.
**Klikwallie,** C. [klíkwali], brass wire, brass armlet.
**Kliminwhit, klemanawit,** C., a lie, falsehood; to lie.
**Klimmin, klimmin-klimmin,** C., soft; fine in substance.
**Klip,** C., deep, sunken.
**Kliskwiss,** C., mat.
**Klohkloh,** C., oysters. See *Chetlo.*
**Klonass,** C. [klonás], perhaps; I do not know; it is doubtful.
**Kohlkohl,** C., mouse. See *Hoolhool.*
**Klone,** C. [klōn], three.
**Klook,** E., crooked.
**Klootchman,** N., woman, female. *Tenas klootchman,* little woman, girl.
**Kloshe,** N., [klōsh], good, well. *Kloshe spose,* well (is it) if. *Kloshe spose nika klatawa?* shall I go? (lit. well, if I go?)
**Kluh,** C., to tear.
**Klukkul,** C., broad or wide, as a plank.

**Ko,** C., to reach, arrive at, attain.
**Koko,** J., to knock. *Koko stick* (knock-tree), woodpecker.
**Kokshut, kokshutl,** N., to break, kill, destroy; broken, destroyed, killed.
**Konaway,** C. [kónawē], all, every. *Konaway kah,* everywhere.
**Koosah,** C., sky.
**Kopa,** formerly **kwapa,** C. [kópa, or kopá], to, in, at, with, towards, of, about, concerning; there.
**Kopet, kwapet,** C. [kopét, kwapét], to stop, leave off; finished; enough. *Kopet tomalla,* day after to-morrow. *Kopet kumtuks* (no longer know), to forget.
**Kow,** C. [kau], to tie, fasten; a parcel, bundle.
**Kull,** C., hard, solid, difficult.
**Kullah,** S. [kŭláh], fence, enclosure.
**Kumtuks,** N., to know, understand; knowledge, acquaintance. *Kopet kumtuks* (cease to know), to forget. *Halo kumtuks* (no understanding), stupid.
**Kunamoxt,** C. [kŭn'amokst], both, together. *Kunamoxt kahkwa,* both alike.
**Kunjik, kunsic, kunjuk,** C., how many, when, ever. *Wake kunjik* (not ever), never.

**Kushis**, S., stockings.
**Kwaddis**, J., whale.
**Kwahta**, E., quarter of a dollar.
**Kwanesum**, C. [kwánisŭm], always, for ever.
**Kwaist**, C. [kwaist, or kwēst], nine.
**Kwalal-kwalal**, C., to gallop.
**Kwahl**, S., aunt.
**Kwan**, C., glad ; tamed.
**Kwass**, C., fear, afraid, tame.
**Kwates, kwehts**, S. [kwēts], sour.
**Kwehkweh**, J., a mallard duck.
**Kwekwiens**, S., a pin.
**Kweokweo**, C., ring, circle.
**Kwinnum**, C., five.
**Kwitl**, C., to shoot, hunt, kill.
**Kwish**, or **kweesh** (exclamation of refusal), pooh ! no indeed !
**Kwitshadie**, S., hare, rabbit.
**Kwolann**, S. [kwolán], the ear.
**Kwulh, hwult**, C., to hit, strike, or wound (without cutting).
**Kwunnum**, S., counting. *Mamook kwunnum*, to count.
**Kwutl**, C., to push, squeeze ; tight, fast.

## L.

**Lableed**, F., a bridle.
**Laboos**, F. [labūs], mouth.
**Labooti**, F. [labutaí], bottle.
**Lacalat**, F. [lakalát], carrot.

**Lacaset**, F. [lacasét], a box, trunk, chest.
**Lacloa**, F., a cross.
**Lah**, v., C., to lean, to tip (as a boat), to stoop, to bend over (as a tree).
**Lagome**, F., pitch, glue, gum.
**Lagween**, a saw.
**Lahash**, F., an axe or hatchet.
**Lake**, E., lake.
**Lakit**, C. [láhkit], four.
**Lakless**, F. [laklés], fat, oil. See *Glease*.
**Lala**, J., long time. *Wake lala*, not long.
**Lalah**, C. [lalá], to cheat, trick, joke with.
**Lalahm**, F., an oar. *Mamook lalahm*, to row.
**Lalang, lalan**, F., the tongue ; language.
**Laleem**, F., a file.
**Lamess**, F., the ceremony of the mass.
**Lamestin, lametchin**, F., medicine, physic.
**Lammieh**, F. [lámiē], an old woman (*la vieille*).
**Lamonti**, F. [lamontai], a mountain.
**Lapeashe**, F. [lapiésh], a trap (*la piège*).
**Lapeep**, F., tobacco-pipe.
**Lapehsh**, F., pole (*la perche*).
**Lapellah**, J. [lapelá], roasted. *Mamook lapellah*, to roast before the fire. See *Appola*.

**Lapell,** F. [lapél], a shovel or spade.
**Lapeosh,** F. [lapiōsh], a mattock, a hoe.
**Laplash,** F., board (*la planche*).
**Lapoel,** F. [lapoél], a stove.
**Lapool,** F., fowl, poultry. *Siwash lapool* (Indian fowl), grouse.
**Lapooshet,** F., fork (*la fourchette*).
**Lapote,** F., door.
**Lasanjel,** F., girth, sash, belt (*la sangle*).
**Lasee,** F., a saw.
**Lasell,** F., saddle.
**Lashalloo,** F. [láshalu], plough (*la charue*).
**Lashandel,** F., candle.
**Lashase,** F. [lashés], chair.
**Lashen,** F. [lashén], a chain.
**Lassiett,** F. [lasiét], a plate.
**Lasway,** F., silk.
**Latahb,** F., table.
**Latet,** F. [latét], the head.
**Latlah,** F. [latlá], noise. (F. *faire du train*, to make a noise.)
**Lawen,** F. [lawén], oats (*l'avoine*).
**Lawest,** F., waistcoat, vest.
**Lazy,** E., lazy.
**Lebardo,** F., shingle (*le bardeau*).
**Lebal,** F. [libál], ball, bullet.
**Lebiskwie,** F., biscuit, crackers, hard bread.

**Lecock,** F., a cock, a fowl.
**Ledoo,** F. [lidú], finger (*le doigt*).
**Lejaub,** F., devil (*le diable*).
**Lekleh,** F. [liklé], key.
**Lekloo,** F., nail.
**Lekoo,** F., neck.
**Lekye,** spot, spotted; a piebald horse.
**Leloba,** F., ribbon (*le ruban*).
**Leloo,** F., wolf.
**Lemah** [limá], or **lehma** [léma], F., hand.
**Lemahto,** F., hammer (*le marteau*).
**Lemel,** F. [limél], mule (*le mulet*).
**Lemolo,** F., wild, untamed (*le marron*).
**Lemooto,** F., sheep.
**Lenay,** F., nose.
**Lepan,** F. [lipán], bread.
**Lepee,** F., foot.
**Lepishemo** [lipíshimo], saddle-housing.
**Leplet,** F. [liplét], priest, minister, missionary (*le prêtre*).
**Lepome,** F. [lipóm], apple.
**Lepwah,** F. [lipwá], peas.
**Lesak,** F. [lisák], bag, pocket.
**Lesap,** F. [lisáp], egg, eggs (*les œufs*).
**Lesook,** F., sugar.
**Letah,** F. [litá], the teeth (*les dents*).
**Lewhet,** F. [lihwét], a whip (*le fouet*).

Lice, E., rice.
Liplip, J., to boil.
Liskwis, C., mat. See *Kliskwiss.*
Lolo, C., to carry, take.
Loloh, C. [loló], round, whole, complete.
Lope, E., rope.
Lum, E., rum, ardent spirits.

### M.

Mahkook, N. [mákuk], to trade, buy or sell; a bargain.
Mahsh, or mash, F., to leave, put away, remove (*marcher*).
Mahsie, F., to thank.
Mahtlinie, C. [mátlini], off shore; (in boating) keep off! (if on land) towards the water.
Mahtwillie, C. [mátwili], in shore, shoreward; keep in! (on land) towards the woods, or inland.
Malah, C. [malá], tinware, earthenware, dishes.
Malieh, F. [malié], to marry.
Mama, E., mother.
Mamook, N. [mámuk], to make, do, work. Used generally as a causative verb, as, *mamook chaco* (make to come), bring; *mamook liplip*, make to boil.
Man, E., man, male. *Tenas man*, young man, boy.
Melass, F., molasses.

Memaloose. See *Mimaloose.*
Mesachie, C. [mesátshi], bad, wicked.
Mesika, C. [misaíka], ye, you, yours.
Mika, C. [maika], thou, thy, thine.
Mimaloose, C., to die; dead. *Mimaloose illahee* (death ground), cemetery, sepulchre.
Mimie, C. [maími], down stream.
Mistchimas, N., slave.
Mitass, J. [mitás], leggings.
Mitlite, C. [mítlait], to sit, stay, reside; to be, have.
Mitwhit, C., to stand. *Mitwhit stick* (standing-tree), mast.
Moxt, C., two, twice. *Moxt poh*, double-barrelled gun.
Moola, F., mill. *Stick moola* (wood mill), saw-mill.
Moon, E., moon.
Moosmoos, C., buffalo.
Moosum, S., to sleep; sleep.
Mowitsh, or mawitsh, N. [mauitsh], deer, wild animal.
Muckamuck, J., food; to eat, bite, drink.
Musket, E., musket, gun.

### N.

Na, or nah, J., the interrogative particle. *Sick na mika?* Are you sick.

**Nah,** or **naah**! J., interj., ho! hey! look here! *Nah sikhs!* halloo, friend!

**Nanitsh, N.** [nánitsh], to see, look, seek.

**Nawitka, C.,** certainly, indeed.

**Nem, E.,** name.

**Nesika, C.** [nisaíka], we, us, our.

**Newha, C.** [níwha], here; come here.

**Nigga, E.,** negro, African.

**Nika, C.** [naíka], I, me, my, mine.

**Nose, E.,** nose; promontory; prow of boat.

### O.

**Okoke,** or **okuk, C.** [ókok], this, that, it.

**Oleman, E.** [óliman], old man; old, worn out.

**Olhiyu, C.** [olhaíyu], a seal (*phoca*).

**Olillie,** or **olallie, C.** [ólili], berries. *Shot olillie*, huckleberries. *Seahpolt olillie* (capberries), raspberries.

**Olo, C.,** hungry, craving. *Olo chuck*, thirsty. *Olo moosum*, sleepy.

**Oluk, S.,** make.

**Ooskan,** or **oiskin, C.,** cup, bowl.

**Owakut, C.,** road. See *Wayhut*.

**Opekwan, C.** [ópikwan], basket; tin kettle.

**Opitlkeh, C.** [ópitlkeh], bow.

**Opitsah, C.** [ópitsah], knife.

**Opoots, C.** [óputs], tail; hinder part; stern of vessel.

**Ow, C.** [au], younger brother.

### P.

**Pahtl, C.,** full. *Pahtl lum*, or *pahtlum* (full of rum), drunk. *Pahtl chuck* (full of water), wet.

**Paint,** or **pent, E.,** paint.

**Papa, E.** and **F.,** father.

**Papeh, E.** [pépah], paper, letter, picture.

**Paseesee, F.,** blanket, woollen cloth (*i.e., Françaises*, French goods).

**Pasiooks, F.** [pasaíooks], French, Frenchmen (from *Français*, with the Chinook plural termination, *uks*).

**Pay, E.,** pay.

**Pechuh,** or **pechuk, C.** [pitshŭh'], green.

**Pe,** or **pee, F.,** and, then, or, but (Fr. *puis*).

**Pehpah.** See *Papeh*.

**Pelton, J.,** a fool, foolish, crazy.

**Peshak,** or **peshuk, N.,** bad.

**Pewhattie, C.,** thin, slight, flimsy.

**Piah, E.,** fire, cooked, ripe. *Mamook piah*, to cook. *Piahship*, steamer.

E

Pil, C., red. *Pil dolla*, gold.
Pilpil, J., blood.
Pish, E., fish.
Pishpish, cat. See *Pusspuss*.
Pitlil, thick, as molasses.
Piupiu, F. [piúpiu], to stink. (Fr. *puer*.)
Poh, J., a puff of breath. *Mamook poh*, to blow out, as a candle, to fire a gun.
Polallie, F. [pólali], gunpowder, dust, sand. (Fr. *poudre*.)
Poolie, F., rotten.
Pos. See *Spose*.
Potlatsh, or pahtlatsh, N., to give; a gift.
Pray, E., to pray.
Pukpuk, J., a blow with the fist.
Pusspuss, or pishpish, E., cat. *Hyas pusspuss*, panther.

## S.

Saghalie, or sahhalie, C. [sáhali], above, up, high; heaven; heavenly. *Saghalie tyee* (heavenly chief), God.
Sail, or sell, E., sail, cotton or linen cloth.
Sakoleks, C. [sakóleks], trousers, leggings.
Salmon, or sahmun, E. [sámŭn], salmon.
Salt, E., salt.
Sapolill, C., wheat, corn, flour, or meal.

Seahhost, or seaghost, C. [siáhost], face, eye, eyes.
Seahpo, or seahpolt, F. [siápo], hat or cap. (Fr. *chapeau*.)
Shame, or shem, E., shame.
Shantie, F., to sing.
Shelokum, C. [shilókam], glass, looking-glass.
Ship, E., ship. *Shipman*, sailor.
Shoes, E., shoes, mocassins. *Stick shoes* (lit. wooden shoes), stiff leathern shoes.
Shot, E., shot, lead.
Shugah, E., sugar.
Shut, E., shirt.
Shwahkuk, E., frog.
Seed, E., seed.
Siah, N. [saiá], far, far off. *Wake siah*, not far, near.
Siam, C. [saíam], the grizzly bear.
Sick, E., sick, sickness. *Sick tumtum*, grieved, sorry, sick at heart.
Sikhs, C., friend.
Sinamoxt, C. [sínamokst], seven.
Sing, E., to sing; song.
Sitkum, C., half, part. *Sitkum dolla*, half-a-dollar. *Sitkum sun*, noon. *Tenas sitkum*, a quarter, or small part.
Sitshum, S. [sít-shum], to swim.
Siwash, F. [saíwash], Indian. (Fr. *sauvage*.)

## DICTIONARY. 51

Skin, E., skin. *Stickskin* (lit. tree-skin), bark.
Skookum, or skookoom, S., strong; a demon, ghost.
Skwiskwis, C., squirrel.
Smoksmok, C., grouse.
Smoke, E., smoke, clouds, fog, steam.
Snass, J., rain. *Cole snass* (cold rain), snow.
Soap, E., soap.
Solleks, or sahleks, J., angry; anger. *Mamook solleks*, to fight.
Sopena, C. [sópina], to jump, leap.
Spoon, E., spoon.
Spose, E., suppose, if, when. (Often pronounced pōs.)
Stick, E., stick, tree, wood; wooden. *Ikt stick*, one yard.
Stocken, E., stocking, sock.
Stoh, C., loose; to untie, set free.
Stone, E., stone, rock, bone, horn.
Stotekin, C. [stótkin], eight.
Stutshin, E., sturgeon.
Sun, E., sun, day. *Tenas sun* (little sun), early morning.
Sunday, E., Sunday. *Ikt Sunday*, one week. *Hias Sunday* (great Sunday), a holiday, Christmas.

### T.

Taghum, or tohum, C., six.
Tahlkie, C., yesterday.
Tahtlum, tahtelum, C., ten.
Takamonuk, C., hundred.
Talapus, C., coyote, prairie wolf.
Talkie, E., speech, discourse. *Sunday talkie*, sermon.
Tamahnowus, C. [tamánowus], luck, fortune, magic; sorcerer.
Tamolitsh, C. [tamólitsh], tub, barrel, bucket.
Tanse, E. or F., dance.
Tahnkie, C., yesterday. See *Tahlkie*.
Tea, E., tea.
Teahwit, C. [tiáwit], leg, foot.
Tenas, or tanas, N. [ténas], small, few, little, young; child.
Tepeh, C. [tepéh], quill, wing.
Tikegh, or takeh, C. [tikéh], to want, wish, love, like.
Tiktik, J., a watch.
Tilikum, or tillikum, C., people.
Till, or tull, E., tired, heavy; weight. (English, *tire*.)
Tintin, J., bell; to ring.
Tipso, C., grass, leaves, fringe, feathers, fur. *Dly tipso*, hay.
T'kope, C., white, light-coloured.
Tl'kope, C., to cut, hew, chop.
Toh, or tooh, J., spitting. *Mamook toh*, to spit.
Tolo, J., to earn, gain, win, conquer.
Tomolla, E., to-morrow.

## 52 THE OREGON TRADE LANGUAGE.

**Tot**, S., uncle.
**Toto**, J., to shake, sift, winnow.
**Totoosh**, J. [totúsh], breast, udder, milk.
**Towagh**, C., bright, shining, light.
**Tsee**, C., sweet.
**Tseepie** [tsipi], to mistake. *Tseepie wayhut*, to take the wrong path.
**Tsikstik**, J., waggon, cart, wheel.
**Tsiltsil**, or **chilchil**, C., buttons; stars.
**Tsolo**, J., to wander, to lose the way.
**Tsugh**, C., a crack or split. *Mamook tsugh*, to split.
**Tukamonuk**, C. [tŭkamónŭk], hundred.
**Tukwilla** [tŭk'willa], nuts.
**Tumchuck**, waterfall. See *Tumwata*.
**Tumtum**, J., the heart; will, mind, feeling, thought, soul; to think, feel.
**Tumwata**, J. and E., waterfall.
**Tupshin**, or **tipsin**, S., needle.
**Tupso**. See *Tipso*.
**Tyee**, N. [taii], chief.
**Tzum**, C., spots, stripes, marks, figures, writing, painting. *Mamook tzum*, to write.

### W.
**Wagh**, C., to pour out; to vomit.
**Wake**, N., no, not.
**Wakut**. See *Wayhut*.
**Wash**, E., to wash.
**Watah**, E., water. See *Chuck* and *Tumwata*.
**Waum**, or **wahm**, E., warm.
**Wawa**, or **wauwau**, N., to talk, speak; speech, talking, word.
**Wayhut**, **wehkut**, **owakut**, C., road, track, path.
**Weght**, or **weht**, C., again, also, more.
**Winapie**, N. [wínapi], soon, presently.
**Wind**, or **win**, E., wind, breath, life.

### Y.
**Yahka**, or **yaka**, C., he, she, it; his, hers, &c.
**Yahwa**, C., there, thither, thence, beyond.
**Yakso**, C., hair.
**Yakwahtin**, C., entrails.
**Yiem**, S. [yaíem], a story, tale; to relate.
**Yootl**, S., pleased, proud.
**Yootlkut**, C., long, length.
**Yootskut**, C., short.
**Yukwa**, or **yakwa**, C., here, hither, this way.

## ENGLISH AND TRADE LANGUAGE.

### A.
Above, *saghalie, sahhalie.*
Across, *inati.*
Afraid, *kwass.*
After, *kimta.*
Again, *weght.*
All, *konaway.*
Always, *kwanesum.*
American, *Boston.*
Amusement, *heehee.*
And, *pe.*
Anger, angry, *solleks.*
Apple, *lepome.*
Arrive, *ko.*
Arrow, *kalitan.*
As, *kahkwa.*
At, *kopa.*
Aunt, *kwalh.*
Axe, *lahash.*

### B.
Bad, *mesachie, peshuk.*
Bag, *lesak.*
Ball, *lebal.*
Bargain, to, *mahkook, huyhuy.*
Bark (of tree), *stickskin.*
Barrel, *tamolitsh.*
Basket, *opekwan.*
Beads, *kamosuk.*
Bear (black), *chetwoot, itswoot;* (grizzly), *siam.*
Beat, to, *kokshut.*

Beaver, *eena.*
Because, *kehwa.*
Bed, *bed.*
Before, *elip.*
Behind, *kimta.*
Bell, *tintin.*
Belly, *yakwahtin.*
Below, *keekwillie.*
Belt, *lasanjel.*
Berries, *olillie.*
Best, *elip kloshe.*
Bird, *kallakala.*
Biscuit, *lebiskwee.*
Bitter, *klihl.*
Black, *klale.*
Blackberries, *klikamuks.*
Blanket, *paseesie.*
Blind, *halo seahhost.*
Blood, *pilpil.*
Blow out, *mamook poh.*
Blue, *klale.*
Blunder, to, *tseepie.*
Board, plank, *laplash.*
Boat, *boat.*
Boil, to, *liplip.*
Bone, *stone.*
Borrow, to, *ayahwhul.*
Both, *kunamoxt.*
Bottle, *labooti.*
Bow, *opitlkegh.*
Bowl, *ooskan.*
Box, *lacaset.*

Bracelet, *klickwallie.*
Brave, *skookum tumtum.*
Bread, *lepan.*
Break, to, *kokshut.*
Breasts, *totoosh.*
Bridle, *lableed.*
Bright, *towagh.*
Broad, *klukulh.*
Broom, *bloom.*
Brother, elder, *kahpo.*
Brother, younger, *ow.*
Brother-in-law, *ekkeh.*
Bucket, *tamolitsh.*
Buffalo, *moosmoos.*
Bullet, *lebal, kalitan.*
Bundle, *kow.*
But, *pe.*
Butter, *totoosh lakless.*
Buttons, *tsiltsil.*
Buy, to, *mahkook.*
By-and-by, *winapie, alkie.*

### C.

Candle, *lashandel, glease piah.*
Carrot, *lacalat.*
Carry, to, *lolo.*
Cart, *tsiktsik.*
Cat, *pusspuss, pishpish.*
Cataract, *tumwata.*
Cattle, *moosmoos.*
Certainly, *nawitka.*
Chain, *lashen, chikamin lope.*
Chair, *lashase.*
Cheat, to, *lalah.*
Chicken, *tenas lapool.*
Chief, *tyee.*
Child, *tenas.*

Clams, *ona.*
Clear up, *chahko klah.*
Cloth (cotton), *sail.*
Cloud, *smoke.*
Coat, *capo.*
Coffee, *caupy.*
Cold, *cole.*
Comb, *comb.*
Come, to, *chahco.*
Confess, to, *yiem.*
Conjuring, *tamahnous.*
Cook, to, *mamook piah.*
Copper, *pil chikamin.*
Cord, *tenas lope.*
Corn, *esalth.*
Cotton cloth, *sail.*
Cough, *hohhoh.*
Count, to, *mamook kwunnum.*
Cousin. See *Sister* and *Brother.*
Coyote, *talapus.*
Crazy, *pelton.*
Cream-coloured, *leclem.*
Crooked, *kiw.t.*
Cross, *lacloa.*
Crow, *kahkah.*
Cry, to, *cly.*
Cup, *ooskan.*
Curly, *hunlkih.*
Cut, to, *tlkope.*

### D.

Dance, to, *tanse.*
Dark, *polaklie.*
Day, *sun.*
Dead, *mimaloose, memaloost.*
Deaf, *ikpooie kwillan.*

Different, *huloima*.
Difficult, *kull*.
Dig, to, *mamook illahie*.
Die, *mimaloose*.
Dime, *bit*, or *mit*.
Do, to, *mamook*.
Doctor, *doctin*.
Dog, *kamooks*.
Dollar, *dolla*, or *tahla*.
Door, *lapote*.
Down stream, *mimie*.
Drink, to, *muckamuck*.
Drive, to, *kishkish*.
Drunk, *pahtlum*.
Dry, *dely*.
Duck, *kwehkweh*.
Dust, *polallie*.

### E.
Eagle, *chakchak*.
Ear, *kwolann*.
Early, *tenas sun*.
Earn, to, *tolo*.
Earth, *illahie*.
Eat, to, *muckamuck*.
Egg, *lesap*, *lezep*.
Eight, *stotekin*.
Elk, *moolock*.
Enclosure, *kullagh*.
English, *Kinchautsh*.
Enough, *hiyu*, *kopet*.
Entrails, *kiyagh*.
Evening, *tenas polaklie*.
Every, *konaway*.
Exchange, *huyhuy*.
Eyes, *seahhost*.

### F.
Face, *seahhost*.
Falsehood, *kliminwhit*.
Far, *siah*.
Fast (quick), *hyak*.
Fast (tight), *kwutl*.
Fasten, to, *kow*.
Fat, *glease*.
Father, *papa*.
Fathom, *itlan*.
Fear, *kwass*.
Fence, *kullagh*.
Fetch, to, *mamook chahko*.
Fever, *waum-sick*.
Few, *tenas*.
Fight, to, *kahdena*, *mamook solleks*.
Fight with fists, *mamook pukpuk*.
Figured (as calico), *tzum*.
File, *laleem*.
Fill, to, *mamook pahtl*.
Find, to, *klap*.
Fingers, *ledoo*.
Fire, *piah*.
First, *elip*.
Fish, *pish*.
Fishhook, *ikkik*.
Five, *kwinnum*.
Flea, *sopen enapoo*.
Flesh, *itlwillie*.
Flint, *kilitsut*.
Flour, *sapolill*.
Fly, to, *kawak*.
Fog, *smoke*.
Food, *muckamuck*.
Fool, foolish, *pelton*.

Foot, *lepee*.
For ever, *kwanesum*.
Forget, to, *mahlie, kopet kumtuks*.
Fork, *lapoushet*.
Formerly, *ahnkuttie*.
Four, *lakit*.
Fowl, *lapool*.
French, *pasiooks*.
Friend, *sikhs*.
Frog, *schwakuk*.
Fry, to, *mamook lapoel*.
Frying-pan, *lapoel*.
Full, *pahtl*.
Fun, *heehee*.

### G.

Gallop, to, *kwalalkwalal*.
Gamble, to, *heehee limah*.
Gather, to, *hokumelh*.
Get, to, *iskum*.
Get out, *mahsh*.
Get up, *get-up*, or *ket-op*.
Ghost, *skookum*.
Gift, *cultus potlatsh*.
Give, to, *potlatsh*.
Glad, *kwann*.
Go, to, *klatawa*.
God, *saghalie tyee*.
Gold, *pil chikamin*.
Good, *kloshe*, or *klose*.
Good-bye, *klahowya*.
Goods, *iktah*.
Goose, *whuywhuy, kalakalahma*.
Grandfather, *chope*.
Grandmother, *chitsh*.

Grass, *tipso*.
Grease, *glease, lakless*.
Green, *pechugh*.
Grey, grey horse, *legley*.
Grizzly bear, *siam*.
Ground, *illahie*.
Grouse, *smoksmok*.
Gun, *musket, sukwalal*.

### H.

Hair, *yakso*.
Half, *sitkum*.
Hammer, *lemahto*.
Hand, *lemah*.
Handkerchief, *hakatshum*.
Hard, *kull*.
Hare, *kwitshadie*.
Harrow, to, *mamook comb illahie*.
Hat, *seahpo, seahpolt*.
Haul, *haul*.
Hay, *dly tipso*.
He, his, *yahka, yaka*.
Head, *latet*.
Heart, *tumtum*.
Heaven, *saghalie illahie*.
Heavy, *till*.
Help, to, *mamook elann*.
Here, *yukwa*.
Hide, to, *ipsoot*.
High, *saghalie, sahhalie*.
Hit, to, *kwul'h*.
Hoe, *lapeosh*.
Hog, *cosho*.
Hole, *klawhap*.
Holiday, *hias sunday*.
Horn, *stone*.

Horse, *kiutan*.
House, *house*.
How, *kahta*.
How are you? *klahowya?*
How many? *kunjik? kunsik?*
Hundred, *tukamonuk*.
Hungry, *olo*.
Hunt, *kwitl*.
Hurry, *howh, hyak*.

### I.

I, *nika*.
If, *spose*.
In, *kopa*.
Indian, *siwash*.
In shore, *mahtwillie*.
Iron, *chikamin*.
It, *yahka*.

### J.

Jealous, *sick tumtum*.
Jump, to, *sopena*.

### K.

Kamass-root, *lakamass*.
Kettle, *ketling*.
Kick, to, *chukkin*.
Kill, to, *mamook mimaloose, kwitl, kokshut*.
Kiss, to, *bebee*.
Knife, *opitsah*.
Knock, to, *koko*.
Knotty, *hunlkih*.
Know, to, *kumtuks*.

### L.

Lake, *lake*.
Lame, *klook teahwit*.

Language, *lalang*.
Large, *hyas*.
Lately, *chee*.
Laugh, *heehee*.
Lazy, *lazy*.
Leap, to, *sopena*.
Leaf, *tipso, tupso*.
Lean, to, *lagh*.
Leave, to, *mahsh*.
Leave off, to, *kopet*.
Leg, *teahwit*.
Leggings, *mitass*.
Lend, to, *ayahwhul*.
Lick, to, *klakwun*.
Lie, to, *kliminwhit*.
Like, *kahkwa*.
Like, to, *tikegh*.
Little, *tenas*.
Long, *youtlkut*.
Long ago, *ahnkuttie*.
Look, to, *nanitsh*.
Look here! *nah*.
Looking-glass, *shelokum*.
Loose, *stoh*.
Lose the way, *tsolo, tseepie wayhut*.
Love, to, *tikegh*.

### M.

Magic, *tamahnowus*.
Maize, *esalth*.
Make, to, *mamook*.
Man, *man*.
Many, *hyu*.
Marry, to, *malieh*.
Mass (ceremony), *lamesse*.
Mast, *shipstick*.

Mat, *kliskwiss*.
Mattock, *lapeosh*.
Measure, to, *tahnim*.
Meat, *itlwillie*.
Medicine, *lamestin*.
Mend, to, *mamook tipolim*.
Metal, *chikamin*.
Middle, *katsuk*.
Midnight, *sitkum polaklie*.
Milk, *totoosh*.
Mill, *moola*.
Mind, the, *tumtum*.
Minister, *leplet*.
Miss, to, *tseepie*.
Missionary, *leplet*.
Mistake, to, *tseepie, tsolo*.
Mocassins, *skinshoes*.
Molasses, *melass*.
Money, *chikamin*.
Month, *moon*.
Moon, *moon*.
More, *weght*.
Mosquito, *melakwa*.
Mother, *mama*.
Mountain, *lamonti*.
Mouse, *hoolhool*.
Mouth, *laboos*.
Much, *hyu*.
Mule, *lemel*.
Musket, *musket*.
Mussels, *toluks*.
My, mine, *nika*.

### N.

Nails, *lecloo*.
Name, *nem*.
Near, *wake siah*.
Neck, *lecoo*.
Needle, *keepwot*.
Negro, *nigga*.
New, *chee*.
Night, *polaklie*.
Nine, *kwaist*, or *kweest*.
No, not, *wake*.
Noise, *latlah*.
None, *halo*.
Nonsense, *cultus wawa*.
Noon, *sitkum sun*.
Nose, *nose, lenay*.
Notwithstanding, *keghtchie*.
Now, *alta*.
Nuts, *tukwilla*.

### O.

Oak, *kull stick*.
Oar, *lalahm, lalum*.
Oats, *lawen*.
Off, *klak*.
Off-shore, *mahtlinnie*.
Oil, *glease*.
Old, *oleman*.
Old woman, *lammieh*.
One, *ikt*.
Open, *hahlakl*.
Opposite to, *inati*.
Or, *pe*.
Order, to, *mahsh tumtum*.
Other, *huloima*.
Our, *nesika*.
Out of doors, *klaghanie*.
Ox, *moosmoos*.
Oyster, *chetlo, kloghklogh*.

## P.

Paddle, *isick*.
Paddle, to, *mamook isick*.
Paint, *pent*.
Paper, *papeh, pehpah*.
Pay, *pay*.
Peas, *lepwah*.
People, *tillikums*.
Perhaps, *klonas*.
Petticoat, *kalakwahtie*.
Piebald, *lekye*.
Pin, *kwekwiens*.
Pipe, *lapeep*.
Pitch, *lagome*.
Plate, *lasiet*.
Pleased, *yootl*.
Plough, *leshalloo*.
Plough, to, *klugh illahie*.
Pole, *lapehsh*.
Poor, *klahowyum, halo ikta*.
Pork, *cosho*.
Potato, *wappatoo*.
Pour, to, *wagh*.
Powder, *polallie*.
Prairie wolf, *talapus*.
Presently, *alkie, winapie*.
Pretty, *toketie*.
Priest, *leplet*.
Proud, *yootl, kwetlh*.
Provided that, *spose*.
Pull, *haul*.

## Q.

Quarter, *tenas sitkum*.
Quarter-dollar, *kwahta*.
Quick, *hyak*.
Quills, *tepeh*.

## R.

Rabbit, *kwitshadie*.
Rain, *snass*.
Rattle, *shugh*.
Rattle-snake, *shugh-opoots*.
Reach, to, *ko*.
Red, *pil*.
Relate, to, *yiem*.
Return, to, *kelapi*.
Ribbon, *leloba*.
Rice, *lice*.
Rifle, *calipeen*.
Ring, a, *kweokweo*.
Ripe, *piah*.
River, *chuck*.
Road, *wayhut, wakot*.
Roan, *sandelie*.
Roast, *mamook lapellah*.
Roasted, *lapellah, appola*.
Rock, *stone*.
Rope, *lope*.
Rotten, *poolie*.
Round, *lolo*.
Rudder, *boat opoots*.
Rum, *lum*.
Run, *cooley, koolie*.

## S.

Sack, *lesak*.
Saddle, *lasell*.
Saddle-housings, *lepishemo*.
Sail, *sail, sel*.
Sailor, *shipman*.
Salmon, *salmon, sahmun*.
Salt, *salt*.
Sand, *polallie*.
Sash, *lasanjel*.

Saw, *lagwin, lasee.*
Say, to, *wawa.*
Scissors, *leseezo.*
Sea, *salt chuck.*
Seal, *olhiyu, siwash cosho.*
See, to, *nanitsh.*
Sell, to, *mahkook.*
Seven, *sinamoxt.*
Sew, to, *mamook tipshin.*
Shake, to, *toto, hullel.*
Shame, *shem.*
Sharp, *yahkisilth.*
Sharpen, to, *mamook tsish.*
She, her, *yahka.*
Sheep, *lemooto.*
Shell-money, small, *coopcoop;* large, *hykwa.*
Shingle, *lebahdo.*
Shining, *towagh.*
Ship, *ship.*
Shirt, *shut.*
Shoes, *shoes.*
Shoot, to, *mamook poo, kwitl.*
Short, *yuteskut.*
Shot, *shot, tenas lebal.*
Shout, to, *hyas wawa.*
Shovel, *lapell.*
Shut, to, *ikpooie.*
Sick, *sick.*
Sift, *toto.*
Silk, *lasway.*
Silver, *t'kope chikamin.*
Similar, *kahkwa.*
Since, *kimta.*
Sing, to, *shantie.*
Sister, elder, *kahp'ho;* younger, *ats.*

Sit, to, *mitlite.*
Six, *toghum.*
Skin, *skin.*
Skunk, *hum opoots.*
Sky, *koosagh.*
Slave, *eliteh, mistshimus.*
Sleep, *moosum.*
Slowly, *klahwa.*
Small, *tenas.*
Smell, a, *humm.*
Smoke, *smoke.*
Snake, *oluk.*
Snow, *snow, cole snass.*
Soap, *soap.*
Soft, *klimmin.*
Sorry, *sick tumtum.*
Soul, *tumtum.*
Sour, *kwates.*
Spade, *lapell.*
Speak, to, *wawa.*
Spill, to, *wagh.*
Spirits, *lum.*
Split, *tsugh.*
Split, to, *mamook tsugh.*
Spectacles, *dolla siahhost.*
Spit, to, *mamook to.*
Spoon, *spoon.*
Spotted, *lekye, tzum.*
Squirrel, *skwiskwis.*
Stab, to, *klemahun.*
Stand, to, *mitwhit.*
Stars, *tsiltsil, klaseess.*
Stay, to, *mitlite.*
Steal, to, *kapsualla.*
Steam, *smoke.*
Steamer, *piah ship.*
Stick, *stick.*

## DICTIONARY. 61

Stink, *piupiu, humm.*
Stirrup, *sitlay.*
Stockings, *stocken, kushis.*
Stone, *stone.*
Stop, *kopet.*
Store, *mahkook house.*
Story, *ekahnam.*
Straight, *delate, sipah.*
Strawberries, *amoteh.*
Strong, *skookum.*
Sturgeon, *stutchun.*
Sugar, *lesook, shugah, shukwa.*
Summer, *waum illahee.*
Sun, *sun.*
Sunday, *Sunday.*
Sunset, *klip sun.*
Suppose, *spose.*
Swan, *kahloke.*
Sweep, to, *mamook bloom.*
Sweet, *tsee.*
Swim, *sitshum.*

### T.

Table, *latahb.*
Tail, *opoots.*
Take, to, *iskum.*
Take care! *klosh nanitsh!*
Take off, or away, *mahsh, mamook klak.*
Tale, story, *yiem, ehkahnem.*
Talk, *wawa, wauwau.*
Tame, *kwass.*
Tea, *tea.*
Teach, to, *mamook kumtuks.*
Tear, to, *klugh.*
Teeth, *letah.*
Tell, to, *wawa.*

Ten, *tahtlum, tahtlelum.*
Thank, *mahsie.*
That, *okoke.*
That way, *yahwa.*
There, *yahwa, kopah.*
They, *klaska.*
Thick (as molasses), *pitlilh.*
Thin (as a board), *pewhattie.*
Thing, *iktah.*
Think, *tumtum.*
This, *okoke.*
This way, *yukwa.*
Thou, they, *mika.*
Thread, *klapite.*
Three, *klone.*
Throw away, *mahsh.*
Tide, high, *saghalie chuck.*
Tide, low, *keekwillie chuck.*
Tie, to, *kow.*
Tight, *kwutl.*
Tinware, *malah.*
Tip, to, *lagh.*
Tired, *till, tull.*
To, towards, *kopa.*
Tobacco, *kinootl, kinoos.*
To-morrow, *tomolla.*
Tongue, *lalang, lalan.*
Trail, track, *waykut.*
Trap, *lapeashe.*
Tree, *stick.*
Tree, fallen, *whim stick.*
Trot, to, *tehtsh.*
Trousers, *sakoleks.*
True, *delate.*
Tub, *tamolitsh.*
Twine, *tenas lope, klapite.*
Two, twice, *mokst.*

## U.

Uncle, *tot*.
Under, *keekwillie*.
Understand, *kumtuks*.
Untamed, *lemolo*.
Untie, *mamook stoh, mahsh kow, mamook klak*.
Up, *saghalie*.
Upset, to, *kelapi*.
Us, *nesika*.

## V.

Venison, *mowitsh*.
Very, *hyas*.
Vessel, *ship*.
Vest, *lawest*.
Vomit, to, *wagh*.

## W.

Waggon, *tsiktsik, chikchik*.
Wander, to, *tsolo*.
Want, to, *tikegh*.
Warm, *waum*.
Wash, to, *mamook wash*.
Watch, a, *tiktik*.
Water, *chuck, wata*.
Waterfall, *tumwata, tumchuck*.
We, *nesika*.
Weigh, to, *mamook till*.
Wet, *pahtl chuck*.
Whale, *ehkolie, kwaddis*.
What, *iktah, kahta*.
Wheat, *sapolill*.
Wheel, *tsiktsik, chikchik*.

When, *kansik, kunjuk*.
Where, *kah*.
Whip, *lewhet*.
White, *t'kope*.
Who, *klaksta*.
Whole, *lolo*.
Why, *kahta*.
Wicked, *mesahchie, peshuk*.
White, *klukulh*.
Wild, *lemolo*.
Will, purpose, *tumtum*.
Willow, *eena-stick*.
Win, to, *tolo*.
Wind, *win, wind*.
Winter, *cole illahie*.
Wipe, to, *klakwun*.
Wire, *chikamin lope*.
Wish, to, *tikegh, tikeh*.
With, *kopa*.
Without (not having), *halo*.
Wolf, *leloo*.
Woman, *klootshman*.
Woman, old, *lamieh*.
Wood, *stick*.
Wooden, *stick*.
Work, to, *mamook*.
Worn out, *oleman*.
Worthless, *cultus*.
Wound, to, *klemahun*.
Write, to, *mamook papeh, mamook tzum*.

## Y.

Year, *ikt cole*.
Yellow, *kawkawak*.

Yes, *ahha, eyeh*.
Yes indeed, *nawitka*.
Yesterday, *tahlkie, tahnkie, ikt sun ahnkuttie*.

You, your (pl.), *mesika*. See *mika*, thy.
Young, *tenas*.

2, WHITE HART STREET,
PATERNOSTER SQUARE, E.C.

# WHITTAKER & CO.'S
## LIST OF
# Classical, Educational, and Technical Works.

## CONTENTS.

| | | | |
|---|---|---|---|
| Atlases | 12 | Latin | 11 |
| Arithmetic | 17 | —— Classics | 4-9 |
| Bibliotheca Classica | 4 | Lower Form Series | 6 |
| Cambridge Greek and Latin Texts | 8 | Mercantile Correspondence | 28 |
| Cambridge Texts with Notes | 7 | Miniature Reference Library | 34 |
| English Language | 12 | Minor Arts and Industries | 3 |
| Euclid | 18 | Miscellaneous Educational Books | 14 |
| French | 18 | Pinnock's Catechisms | 15 |
| —— French Series | 21 | Russian | 27 |
| —— French Classics | 21 | Science | 30 |
| —— Mercantile Correspondence | 28 | Shakespeare | 13 |
| —— Modern French Authors | 22 | Spanish | 27 |
| German | 22 | Specialist's Series | 28 |
| —— German Classics | 24 | Students' Editions of the Gospels and the Acts | 11 |
| —— Mercantile Correspondence | 28 | Technical School and College Building | 32 |
| —— Modern German Authors | 24 | Technological Dictionaries | 31 |
| Grammar School Classics | 5 | Whittaker's Library of Arts. etc. | 30 |
| Greek | 10 | | |
| Greek Classics | 4-9 | | |
| Italian | 26 | | |

*Dec.*, 1889.

## Mr. Leland's Educational Publications.

*Third Edition, Crown 8vo, Cloth, 6s.*

# PRACTICAL EDUCATION.

### A WORK ON
### PREPARING THE MEMORY, DEVELOPING QUICKNESS OF PERCEPTION, AND TRAINING THE CONSTRUCTIVE FACULTIES.

### By CHARLES G. LELAND.

*Author of "The Minor Arts," "Twelve Manuals of Art Work," "The Album of Repoussé Work," Industrial Art in Education, or Circular No. 4, 1882," "Hints on Self-Education," etc.*

Mr. LELAND was the first person to introduce *Industrial Art* as a branch of education in the public schools of America. The Bureau of Education at Washington, observing the success of his work, employed him in 1862 to write a pamphlet showing how hand-work could be taken or taught in schools and families. It is usual to issue only 15,000 of these pamphlets, but so great was the demand for this that in two years after its issue more than 60,000 were given to applicants. This work will be found greatly enlarged in "Practical Education." Owing to it thousands of schools, classes, or clubs of industrial art were established in England, America and Austria. As at present a great demand exists for information as to organizing Technical Education, this forms the first part of the work. In it the author indicates that all the confusion and difference of opinion which at present prevails as to this subject, may very easily be obviated by simply beginning by teaching the youngest the easiest arts of which they are capable, and by thence gradually leading them on to more advanced work.

"The basis of Mr. Leland's theory," says a reviewer, "is that before learning, children should acquire the art of learning. It is not enough to fill the memory, memory must first be created. By training children to merely memorize, extraordinary power in this respect is to be attained in a few months. With this is associated exercises in quickness of perception, which are at first purely mechanical, and range from merely training the eye to mental arithmetic, and problems in all branches of education. Memory and quickness of perception blend in the development of the constructive faculties or hand-work Attention or interest is the final factor in this system."

"*Mr. Leland's book will have a wide circulation. It deals with the whole subject in such a downright practical fashion, and is so much the result of long personal experience and observation, as to render it a veritable mine of valuable suggestions.*"—BRITISH ARCHITECT.

"*It has little of the dryness usually associated with such books; and no teacher can read its thoughtful pages without imbibing many valuable ideas.*"—SCOTTISH EDUCATIONAL NEWS.

"*Strongly to be recommended.*"—CHEMICAL NEWS.

"*This valuable little work.*"—LIVERPOOL DAILY POST.

"*Many of Mr. Leland's suggestions might be carried out advantageously among the young folks in our large towns and villages.*"—NORTHERN WHIG.

## Minor Arts and Industries.

A SERIES OF ILLUSTRATED AND PRACTICAL MANUALS FOR SCHOOL USE AND SELF-INSTRUCTION.

EDITED BY CHARLES G. LELAND.

This series of manuals on "The Minor Arts and Industries" is designed on the lines laid down in Mr. Leland's treatise on education. Each handbook will present the subject with which it deals in a thoroughly popular and practical manner; the lessons carry the student on his road step by step from the veriest elements to the point where the most advanced works fitly find their place in his course of study; in short, the greatest pains are taken to ensure a thorough mastery of the rudiments of each subject, and to so clearly state each lesson, illustrating it where necessary by plans and drawings, that even very young children may be interested in and trained to practical work. On similar grounds the self-taught student will find these manuals an invaluable aid to his studies.

*Part* I *now ready, Paper cover,* 1s. *or in cloth,* 1s. 6d.

## DRAWING AND DESIGNING:

IN A SERIES OF LESSONS, WITH NUMEROUS ILLUSTRATIONS,

BY CHARLES G. LELAND, M.A., F.R.L.S.

WOOD CARVING: with numerous illustrations, chiefly from original designs. By CHARLES G. LELAND. [*In the Press.*

Other volumes will follow at intervals, amongst the subjects of which may be named—

| MODELLING. | METAL WORK. |
| LEATHER WORK. | CARPENTERING. |

# GREEK AND LATIN.
## Bibliotheca Classica.

*A Series of Greek and Latin Authors, with English Notes, edited by eminent Scholars. 8vo.*

**ÆSCHYLUS.** By F. A. Paley, M.A. 8s.

**CICERO'S ORATIONS.** By G. Long, M.A. 4 vols. 8s. each.

**DEMOSTHENES.** By R. Whiston, M.A. 2 vols. 8s. each.

**EURIPIDES.** By F. A. Paley, M.A. 3 vols. 8s. each.

**HERODOTUS.** By Rev. J. W. Blakesley, B.D. 2 vols. 12s.

**HESIOD.** By F. A. Paley, M.A. 5s.

**HOMER.** By F. A. Paley, M.A. Vol. I. 8s. Vol. II. 6s.

**HORACE.** By Rev. A. J. Macleane, M.A. 8s.

**JUVENAL AND PERSIUS.** By Rev. A. J. Macleane, M.A. 6s.

**LUCAN.** The Pharsalia. By C. E Haskins, M.A., and W. E. Heitland, M.A. 14s.

**PLATO.** By W. H. Thompson, D.D. 2 vols. 5s. each.

**SOPHOCLES.** Vol. I. By Rev. F. H. Blaydes, M.A. 8s.

———— Vol. II. Philoctetes—Electra—Ajax and Trachiniæ. By F. A. Paley, M.A. 6s.

**TACITUS:** The Annals. By the Rev. P. Frost. 8s.

**TERENCE.** By E. St. J. Parry, M.A. 9s.

**VIRGIL.** By J. Conington, M.A. 3 vols. 10s. 6d. each.

\*\*\* In some cases the volumes cannot be sold separately. The few copies that remain are reserved for complete sets, which may be obtained, at present, for 9l.

## Grammar School Classics.

*A Series of Greek and Latin Authors, with English Notes. Fcap. 8vo.*

**CÆSAR:** DE BELLO GALLICO. By George Long, M.A. 4s.
—— Books I.-III. For Junior Classes. By George Long, M.A. 1s. 6d.
—— Books IV. and V. in 1 vol. 1s. 6d.
—— Books VI. and VII. in 1 vol. 1s. 6d.

**CATULLUS, TIBULLUS, AND PROPERTIUS.** Selected Poems. With Life. By Rev. A. H. Wratislaw. 2s. 6d.

**CICERO:** DE SENECTUTE, DE AMICITIA, and SELECT EPISTLES. By George Long, M.A. 3s.

**CORNELIUS NEPOS.** By Rev. J. F. Macmichael. 2s.

**HOMER:** ILIAD. Books I.-XII. By F. A. Paley, M.A. 4s. 6d.
Books I.-VI., 2s. 6d.; Books VII.-XII., 2s. 6d.

**HORACE.** With Life. By A. J. Macleane, M.A. 3s. 6d. In 2 Parts: Odes, 2s.; Satires and Epistles, 2s.

**JUVENAL:** SIXTEEN SATIRES. By H. Prior, M.A. 3s. 6d.

**MARTIAL:** SELECT EPIGRAMS. With Life. By F. A. Paley, M.A. 4s. 6d.

**OVID:** The FASTI. By F. A. Paley, M.A. 3s. 6d.
—— Books I. and II. in 1 vol. 1s. 6d.
—— Books III. and IV. in 1 vol. 1s. 6d.
—— Books V. and VI. in 1 vol. 1s. 6d.

**SALLUST:** CATILINA and JUGURTHA. With Life. By G. Long, M.A., and J. G. Frazer. 3s. 6d. Catilina, 2s. Jugurtha, 2s.

**TACITUS:** GERMANIA and AGRICOLA. By Rev. P. Frost. 2s. 6d.

**VIRGIL:** BUCOLICS, GEORGICS, and ÆNEID, Books I.-IV. Abridged from Professor Conington's edition. 4s. 6d.

———— ÆNEID, Books V.-XII.   4s. 6d.
*Also in 9 separate volumes*, 1s. 6d. *each.*

**XENOPHON:** The ANABASIS. With Life. By Rev. J. F. Macmichael. 3s. 6d.
*Also in 4 separate volumes*, 1s. 6d. *each.*

———— The CYROPÆDIA.   By G. M. Gorham, M.A. 3s. 6d.

———— Books I. and II. in 1 vol.   1s. 6d.

———— Books V. and VI. in 1 vol.   1s. 6d.

———— MEMORABILIA.   By Percival Frost, M.A. 3s.

**A GRAMMAR-SCHOOL ATLAS OF CLASSICAL GEOGRAPHY,** containing Ten selected Maps. Imperial 8vo. 3s.

*Uniform with the Series.*

**THE NEW TESTAMENT,** in Greek. With English Notes, &c. By Rev. J. F. Macmichael. 4s. 6d. Separate parts, St. Matthew, St. Mark, St. Luke, St. John, Acts, 6d. each, sewed.

## Lower Form Series.

*With Notes and Vocabularies.*

**ECLOGÆ LATINÆ ;** OR, FIRST LATIN READING-BOOK, WITH ENGLISH NOTES AND A DICTIONARY. By the late Rev. P. Frost, M.A. New Edition. Fcap. 8vo. 1s. 6d.

**LATIN VOCABULARIES FOR REPETITION.** By A. M. M. Stedman, M.A. 2nd Edition, revised. Fcap. 8vo. 1s. 6d.

**EASY LATIN PASSAGES FOR UNSEEN TRANSLATION.** By A. M. M. Stedman, M.A. Fcap. 8vo. 1s. 6d.

## Classical and Educational Works. 7

**VIRGIL'S ÆNEID.** Book I. Abridged from Conington's Edition by Rev. J. G. Sheppard, D.C.L. With Vocabulary by W. F. R. Shilleto. 1s. 6d. [*Now ready.*

**CÆSAR : DE BELLO GALLICO.** Book I. With Notes by George Long, M.A., and Vocabulary by W. F. R. Shilleto. 1s. 6d. [Book II. *in the press.*

**TALES FOR LATIN PROSE COMPOSITION.** With Notes and Vocabulary. By G. H. Wells, M.A. 2s.

**MATERIALS FOR LATIN PROSE COMPOSITION.** By the late Rev. P. Frost, M.A. New Edition. Fcap. 8vo. 2s. Key (for Tutors only), 4s.

**A LATIN VERSE-BOOK.** AN INTRODUCTORY WORK ON HEXAMETERS AND PENTAMETERS. By the late Rev. P. Frost, M.A. New Edition. Fcap. 8vo. 2s. Key (for Tutors only), 5s.

**ANALECTA GRÆCA MINORA,** with INTRODUCTORY SENTENCES, ENGLISH NOTES, AND A DICTIONARY. By the late Rev. P. Frost, M.A. New Edition. Fcap. 8vo. 2s.

**GREEK TESTAMENT SELECTIONS.** By A. M. M. Stedman, M.A. 2nd Edition, enlarged, with Notes and Vocabulary. Fcap. 8vo. 2s. 6d.

## Cambridge Texts with Notes.

*A Selection of the most usually read of the Greek and Latin Authors, Annotated for Schools. Fcap. 8vo, 1s. 6d. each, with exceptions.*

**EURIPIDES.** ALCESTIS — MEDEA — HIPPOLYTUS—HECUBA—BACCHÆ—ION (2s.)—ORESTES—PHOENISSÆ—TROADES—HERCULES FURENS—ANDROMACHE — IPHIGENIA IN TAURIS—SUPPLICES. By F. A. Paley, M.A., LL.D.

**ÆSCHYLUS.** PROMETHEUS VINCTUS—SEPTEM CONTRA THEBAS—AGAMEMNON—PERSÆ—EUMENIDES—CHŒPHORŒ. By F. A. Paley, M.A., LL.D.

**SOPHOCLES. ŒDIPUS TYRANNUS—ŒDIPUS COLONEUS—ANTIGONE—ELECTRA—AJAX.** By F. A. Paley, M.A., LL.D.

**THUCYDIDES.** BOOK IV. By. F. A. Paley, M.A., LL.D.

**XENOPHON.** HELLENICA. BOOK II. By Rev. L. D. Dowdall, M.A.

—— ANABASIS. Edited by Rev. J. F. Macmichael. *New edition,* revised by J. E. Melhuish, M.A. In 6 vols. Book I. (with Life, Introduction, Itinerary, &c.); Books II. and III. 2s. ; Book IV., Book V., Book VI., Book VII.

**HOMER.** ILIAD. BOOK I. By F. A. Paley, M.A., LL.D. 1s.

**VIRGIL** (abridged from Conington's edition). BUCOLICS: GEORGICS, 2 parts : ÆNEID, 9 parts.

**TERENCE.** ANDRIA—HAUTON TIMORUMENOS—PHORMIO—ADELPHOE. By Professor Wagner, Ph.D.

**CICERO.** DE SENECTUTE—DE AMICITIA—EPISTOLÆ SELECTÆ. By G. Long, M.A.

**OVID.** SELECTIONS. By A. J. Macleane, M.A.

*Others in preparation.*

## Cambridge Greek and Latin Texts.

These Texts, which are clearly printed at the Cambridge University Press, on good paper, and bound in a handy form, have been reduced in price, and will now meet the requirements of masters who wish to use Text and Notes separately.

**ÆSCHYLUS.** By F. A. Paley, M.A. 2s.

**CÆSAR:** DE BELLO GALLICO. By G. Long, M.A. 1s. 6d.

**CICERO:** DE SENECTUTE et DE AMICITIA, et EPISTOLÆ SELECTÆ. By G. Long, M.A. 1s. 6d.

**CICERONIS ORATIONES.** Vol. I. (in Verrem.) By G. Long, M.A. 2*s.* 6*d.*

**EURIPIDES.** By F. A. Paley, M.A. 3 vols., each 2*s.*

———— Vol. I. Rhesus—Medea—Hippolytus—Alcestis—Heraclidæ—Supplices—Troades—Index.

———— Vol. II. Ion—Helena—Andromache—Electra—Bacchæ—Hecuba—Index.

———— Vol. III. Hercules Furens—Phœnissæ—Orestes—Iphigenia in Tauris—Iphigenia in Aulide—Cyclops—Index.

**HERODOTUS.** By J. G. Blakesley, B.D. 2 vols., each 2*s.* 6*d.*

**HOMERI ILIAS.** I.-XII. By F. A. Paley, M.A. 1*s.* 6*d.*

**HORATIUS.** By A. J. Macleane, M.A. 1*s.* 6*d.*

**JUVENAL ET PERSIUS.** By A. J. Macleane, M.A. 1*s.* 6*d.*

**LUCRETIUS.** By H. A. J. Munro, M.A. 2*s.*

**SALLUSTI CRISPI CATILINA ET JUGURTHA.** By G. Long, M.A. 1*s.* 6*d.*

**SOPHOCLES.** By F. A. Paley, M.A. 2*s.* 6*d.*

**TERENTI COMŒDIÆ.** By W. Wagner, Ph.D. 2*s.*

**THUCYDIDES.** By J. G. Donaldson, D.D. 2 vols., each 2*s.*

**VERGILIUS.** By J. Conington, M.A. 2*s.*

**XENOPHONTIS EXPEDITIO CYRI.** By J. F. Macmichael, B.A. 1*s.* 6*d.*

**NOVUM TESTAMENTUM GRÆCE.** By F. H. Scrivener, M.A. 4*s.* 6*d.* An edition with wide margin for notes, half bound, 12*s.*

## Annotated Editions.

**CICERO'S** MINOR WORKS. De Officiis, &c. &c. With English Notes, by W. C. Tylor, LL.D. 12mo. cloth, 3s. 6d.

**VIRGIL'S** ÆNEID. With English Notes, by C. Anthon, LL.D. Adapted for use in English Schools by the Rev. F. Metcalfe, M.A. *New Edition.* 12mo. 7s. 6d.

## Greek Class Books.

**BEATSON'S** PROGRESSIVE EXERCISES ON THE COMPOSITION OF GREEK IAMBIC VERSE. 12mo. cloth, 3s.

**DAWSON'S** GREEK-ENGLISH LEXICON TO THE NEW TESTAMENT. *New Edition,* by Dr. Tylor. 8vo. cloth, 9s.

**NOVUM TESTAMENTUM GRÆCE.** Textus Stephanici, 1550. Accedunt variæ Lectiones editionum Bezæ, Elzeviri, Lachmanni, Tischendorfii, Tregellesii, curante F. H. Scrivener, M.A. 4s. 6d. An Edition with wide margin for MS. Notes, 4to. half-bound morocco, 12s.

―――― Textûs Stephanici, A.D. 1550, Cum variis Lectionibus Editionum Bezæ, Elzeviri, Lachmanni, Tischendorfii, Tregellesii, Westcott-Hortii, Versionis Anglicanæ Emendatorum, Curante F. H. A. Scrivener, A.M., D.C.L., LL.D., Accedunt Parallela S. Scripturæ Loca. Small post 8vo. cloth, pp. xvi.-598, 7s. 6d.

EDITIO MAJOR *containing, in addition to the matter in the other Edition, the Capitula (majora et minora) and the Eusebian Canons, the various Readings of Westcott and Hort, and those adopted by the Revisers; also a revised and much-enlarged series of References.*

―――― VALPY'S. For the use of Schools. 12mo. cloth, 5s.

―――― Edited by Rev. Macmichael. *See Grammar School Classics.*

## Students' Editions of the Gospels and the Acts.

*Crown 8vo. cloth.*

**THE GOSPEL OF S. MATTHEW.** The Greek Text, with Critical, Grammatical, and Explanatory Notes, &c., by the late Rev. W. Trollope, M.A., re-edited by the Rev. W. H. Rowlandson, M.A. 5s.

**GOSPEL OF S. MARK.** The Greek Text, with Critical, Grammatical, and Explanatory Notes, Prolegomena, &c., by Rev. W. H. Rowlandson, M.A. 4s. 6d.

**GOSPEL OF S. LUKE.** The Greek Text, with Critical, Grammatical, and Explanatory Notes, &c., by the late Rev. W. Trollope, M.A., revised and re-edited by the Rev. W. H. Rowlandson, M.A. 5s.

**ACTS OF THE APOSTLES.** The Greek Text, with Critical, Grammatical, and Explanatory Notes, and Examination Questions, by Rev. W. Trollope, M.A., re-edited and revised by the Rev. G. F. Browne, M.A. 5s.

## Latin Class Books.

**BEDFORD'S PROPRIA QUÆ MARIBUS;** or, Short Rules for the Genders of Latin Nouns, and a Latin Prosody. 12mo. 1s.

**BOSSUT'S LATIN WORD BOOK;** or, First Step to the Latin Language. 18mo. 1s.

────── **LATIN PHRASE BOOK.** 18mo. 1s.

**FLORILEGIUM POETICUM.** A Selection of Elegiac Extracts from Ovid and Tibullus. *New edition*, greatly enlarged with English Notes. By the late Rev. P. Frost, M.A. Fcap. 8vo. 2s.

**GRADUS AD PARNASSUM;** sive novus sinonymorum, epithetorum, versuum, ac phrasium poeticarum, thesaurus. *New edition.* By G. Pyper. 12mo. cloth, 7s.

────── BY VALPY. Whittaker's Improved edition. Latin and English. *New edition.* Royal 12mo. 7s. 6d.

**STODDART'S** NEW DELECTUS; or, Easy Steps to Latin Construing. For the use of Pupils commencing the Language. Adapted to the best Latin Grammars, with a Dictionary attached. *New edition.* 12mo. 4*s.*

**PENROSE'S (REV. JOHN)** Easy Exercises in Latin Elegiac Verse. *New edition.* 12mo. cloth, 2*s.*

—— Key to ditto, for Tutors only, 3*s.* 6*d.*

## Atlases.

**LONG'S** ATLAS OF CLASSICAL GEOGRAPHY. Containing Twenty-four Maps. Constructed by William Hughes, F.R.G.S., and Edited by George Long, M.A. *New edition*, with Coloured Outlines, and an Index of Places. Royal 8vo. 6*s.*

**LONG'S** GRAMMAR SCHOOL ATLAS OF CLASSICAL GEOGRAPHY. Containing Ten Maps, selected from the larger Atlas. Constructed by W. Hughes, F.R.G.S., and edited by George Long, M.A. *New edition*, with Coloured Outlines. Royal 8vo. 3*s.*

## English Language and Miscellaneous.

**ALLEN AND CORNWELL'S** SCHOOL GRAMMAR. Cloth, 1*s* 9*d.*

—— GRAMMAR FOR BEGINNERS. Cloth, 1*s.*

**BELL'S** MODERN READER AND SPEAKER. A Selection of Poetry and Prose, from the Writings of Eminent Authors. 12mo. 3*s.* 6*d.*

**DUNCAN'S** ENGLISH EXPOSITOR; or, Explanatory Spelling-book. Containing an Alphabetical Collection of all the most useful, proper, and elegant words in the English language, divided into Syllables, and properly accented. *New edition.* 12mo. 1*s.* 6*d.*

**LATHAM'S (R. G.)** DICTIONARY OF THE ENGLISH LANGUAGE. Abridged and condensed into one volume. 8vo. cloth, 14*s.*

## Classical and Educational Works. 13

**MACKAY (C.) A DICTIONARY OF LOWLAND**
SCOTCH. By Charles Mackay, LL.D. With an Introductory Chapter on the Poetry, Humour, and Literary History of the Scottish Language, and an Appendix of Scottish Proverbs. Large post 8vo. cloth, 7s. 6d. half bound, 8s. 6d.

—— SELECTED POEMS AND SONGS OF CHARLES MACKAY, LL.D. With a Commendatory and Critical Introduction by Eminent Writers. Wide foolscap 8vo. half cloth boards, 1s. 6d. Sewed, 1s.

**WEBSTER'S** DICTIONARY OF THE ENGLISH LANGUAGE. Including Scientific, Technical, and Biblical Words and Terms. *New edition*, with Supplement of over 4,600 New Words and Meanings. 4to. cloth, 1l. 1s.; half-calf, 1l. 10s. With Appendices, £1 11s. 6d.; half-calf, 2l.

---

**SHAKESPEARE'S** PLAYS, with Text and Introduction in English and German. Edited by C. Sachs, Prof. Ph D. 8vo. cloth, each Play or Number, 10d.

*Now Ready:*

1. Julius Cæsar.
2. Romeo and Juliet.
3. King Henry VIII.
4. King Lear.
5. Othello
6. Hamlet.
7. A Midsummer Night's Dream.
8. Macbeth.
9. King John.
10. King Richard II.
11. King Henry IV. I.
12.   „     „    II.
13. King Henry V.
14. King Richard III.
15. Cymbeline.
16. Coriolanus.
17. Antony and Cleopatra.
18. Merchant of Venice.
19. Much Ado about Nothing.

*Others to follow.*

"This edition will be quite a godsend to grown-up students of either language, for the ordinary class reading books are too childish to arrest their attention. The parallel paging saves the labour of using a dictionary, and the series is so low in price as to place it within the reach of all."
*Saturday Review.*

**SHAKESPEARE** REPRINTS. 1. King Lear. Parallel Texts of Quarto 1 and Folio 1. Edited by Dr. W. Vietor, of Marburg. Square 16mo. cloth, 3s. 6d.

*The texts of the first quarto and folio, with collations from the later quartos and folios, are here printed in a compact and convenient volume, intended as a class-book in the University.*

## Miscellaneous Educational Books.

**SEIDEL (ROBT.)** INDUSTRIAL EDUCATION : A Pedagogic and Social Necessity. Crown 8vo. 4s.

**WOODWARD (C.M.)** THE MANUAL TRAINING SCHOOL, ITS AIMS, METHODS, AND RESULTS. With Figured Drawings of Shop Exercises in Woods and Metals. 8vo. 10s.

**BIBLIOGRAPHY OF EDUCATION.** Hints toward a Select and Descriptive Bibliography of Education. Arranged by Topics, and Indexed by Authors. By G. Stanley Hall, Professor, John Hopkins University, and John M. Mansfield. Post 8vo. cloth, pp. xvi.-309, 7s. 6d.

**CHEPMELL'S (REV. DR.)** SHORT COURSE OF GRECIAN, ROMAN, AND ENGLISH HISTORY. *New edition.* 12mo. 5s. Questions on, 12mo. 1s.

**COLTON (B. P.)** ELEMENTARY COURSE OF PRACTICAL ZOOLOGY. By B. P. Colton, A.M., Instructor in Biology, Ottawa High School. Crown 8vo. cloth, pp. xiv.-182, 4s. 6d.

**CORNWELL'S** SCHOOL GEOGRAPHY. 3s. 6d. With Thirty Maps on Steel, 5s. 6d.

—— GEOGRAPHY FOR BEGINNERS. 1s. With Questions, 1s. 4d.

**DURHAM UNIVERSITY CALENDAR**, with Almanack. Cloth, 1s. 6d. [*Published annually.*

**JOYCE (P. W.)** A HANDBOOK OF SCHOOL MANAGEMENT AND METHODS OF TEACHING. By P. W. Joyce, LL.D., &c. 11*th edition, revised.* Cloth, 3s. 6d.

**A NATURE READER.** Seaside and Wayside. By Julia McNair Wright. Cloth, 1s. 6d.
    An elementary Reader for young children, designed to instil a love of Natural History. It treats of crabs, wasps, spiders, bees, and some univalve molluscs.

## Classical and Educational Works. 15

**PINNOCK'S** HISTORY OF ENGLAND. From the Invasion of Julius Cæsar. With a Biographical and Historical Dictionary. Questions for Examination, Genealogical Tables, Progress of Literature and the Constitution, &c. Illusted. Continued by the Rev. W. H. Pinnock, LL.D. *New edition.* 12mo. 6s.

—— HISTORY OF GREECE. With an Introduction on the Natural and Political Geography of Greece, Dictionary of Difficult Terms, Questions for Examination, Genealogical Tables, &c. Illustrated. By Dr. W. C. Taylor. *New edition.* 12mo. 5s. 6d.

—— HISTORY OF ROME. With an Introduction, the Geography of the Roman Empire, Notices of the Roman Manners, and Illustrations, Questions for Examination, Chronological Index, &c Illustrated. By Dr. W. C. Taylor. *New edition.* 12mo. 5s. 6d.

**PINNOCK'S** CATECHISMS OF THE ARTS, SCIENCES, AND LITERATURE Whittaker's Improved Editions. Illustrated with Maps, Plates, and Woodcuts, carefully re-edited. 18mo. price 9d. each.

HISTORY.—Modern—Ancient—Universal—Bible and Gospel—Scripture—Chronology— England—Scotland— France—America—Rome—Greece—Jews.

GEOGRAPHY.—Ancient—Modern, Improved Edition—Modern, Original Edition—Sacred—England and Wales—Use of the Globes.

GRAMMAR —English—French—German— Italian— Latin—Spanish—Greek: Part I. Accidence. Part II. Syntax and Prosody—Hebrew.

MATHEMATICS, &c.—Algebra (two Parts)—Arithmetic—Geometry—Navigation—Land Surveying

RELIGION.—Religion—Natural Theology—Scripture History—Bible and Gospel History.

FINE ARTS, &c.—Architecture—Drawing—Perspective—Music—Singing.

LITERATURE.— Mythology— Rhetoric— Logic— British Biography—Classical Biography.

MISCELLANEOUS.—First Catechism—General Knowledge—Intellectual Philosophy—Agriculture—English Law—Heraldry—Medicine—Moral and Social Duties—Trade and Commerce.

**SCHLEYER'S GRAMMAR**, with Vocabularies of Volapuk (the Language of the World), for all Speakers of the English Language. Second (greatly Revised) Edition. By W. A. Seret, Certificated Teacher of the Universal Language. Crown 8vo. pp. 420, sewed, 5s. 6d.; cloth, 6s. 6d.

**SHUMWAY (E. S.) A DAY IN ANCIENT ROME.** With numerous Illustrations. By Edgar S. Shumway, Professor, Rutger's College, New Brunswick. Small 4to. cloth, 5s.

**WATTON'S ORIGINAL AIDS TO EDUCATION.**

Hand-series of Tablets, in Stiff Covers, 3d. each.

Leading Events of General History.
Chief Events of Old Testament History.
Chief Events of New Testament History.
Prophecies and other Scripture Subjects.
Chief Events of Grecian History.
Chief Events of Roman History.
Chief Events of Eastern Empire.
Chief Events of German History.
Chief Events of English History.
Chief English Battles and Results.
Chief Events of Scottish History.
Chief Events of French History.
Chief Events of Prussian History.
Chief Events of Russian History.
Eminent Men of Modern Times.
Chief Events of Church History.
Natural System of Botany.
The Linnæan System of Botany.
Natural History—Zoology.
Natural Philosophy.
Principles of Grammatical Analysis, with Examples.
Guide to English Parsing, with Examples.
Abstract of Heathen Mythology.
Word Formation—Saxon, Latin, and Greek Prefixes, with Examples.
Chief Grecian and Roman Battles and Results.

LARGE TYPE SERIES OF TABLETS

(20 by 23 inches), embracing Historical, Geographical, and other Subjects, 4d. each, for suspension.

WATTON'S SKELETON EXERCISE BOOKS.

For History, Geography, Biography, Analysis, Parsing, and Chronology, with Script Headings and Specimen Page. Price regulated by the thickness of the books, 1s. and 2s. each.
Also now ready, a filled Biographical Exercise Book, 2 Series, each 1s. Charts systematically arranged with date words, 60 pages, cloth, 1s. Selected Descriptive Poetry, 1s.
Object Lessons, Nos. 1, 2, 3, and 4, 32 pp., in stiff covers, 2d. each.

## School and University Analyses.

By the Rev. Dr. Pinnock.

**AN ANALYSIS OF SCRIPTURE HISTORY**; Intended for Readers of Old Testament History, and the University Examinations; with Maps, Copious Index, and Examination Questions. 18mo. cloth, 3s. 6d.

**AN ANALYSIS OF NEW TESTAMENT HISTORY**; Embracing the Criticism and Interpretation of the original Text; with Questions for Examination. 18mo. cloth, 4s.

**AN ANALYSIS OF ECCLESIASTICAL HISTORY**; From the Birth of Christ, to the Council of Nice, A.D. 325. With Examination Questions. 18mo. cloth, 3s. 6d.

**ANALYSIS OF ENGLISH CHURCH HISTORY**; comprising the Reformation period, and subsequent events; with Questions of Examination, especially intended for the Universities and Divinity Students in general. 18mo. cloth, 4s. 6d.

**A SHORT ANALYSIS OF OLD TESTAMENT HISTORY.** With Questions for Schools. 18mo. cloth, 1s. 6d.

**A SHORT ANALYSIS OF NEW TESTAMENT HISTORY.** With Questions for Schools. 18mo. cloth, 1s. 6d.

## Arithmetic and Euclid.

**PINNOCK'S ARITHMETICAL TABLES OF MONEY, WEIGHTS, AND MEASURES.** With Questions for Examination, and Explanatory Notes, &c. 18mo. 3d.

——— **FIRST CIPHERING BOOK.** Containing Easy Exercises in the First Rules of Arithmetic. 4to. sewed, 1s.

**RYAN'S CIVIL SERVICE ARITHMETICAL EXAMINATION PAPERS.** By L. J. Ryan. Cloth, 2s.

——— Key to Ditto. 1s. 6d.

**SONNENSCHEIN AND NESBITT'S ARITHMETIC.** The Science and Art of Arithmetic for the use of Schools. Post 8vo. 5s. 6d. Or separately, Part I.—Integral. 2s. 6d. Parts II. and III.—Fractional and Approximate Calculations. 3s. 6d. Answers to the Exercises. 1s. 6d. Exercises separately. Part I. 1s. Parts II. and III. 1s. 3d.

────── A B C OF ARITHMETIC. Teacher's Book, Nos. 1 and 2, each 1s. Exercise Book, Nos. 1 and 2, each 4d.

**WALKINGAME'S TUTOR ASSISTANT (FRASER'S).** Being a Compendium of Arithmetic and a Complete Question Book. 12mo. 2s. Key, 3s.

**EUCLID, THE FIRST BOOK OF.** With an Introduction and Collection of Problems for the use of Schools. By J. M. Wilson, M.A. 2nd edition. 4to. 2s.

**EUCLID, THE FIRST SIX BOOKS,** together with the ELEVENTH and TWELFTH. From the Text of Dr. Simson. *New edition*, revised and corrected by S. Maynard. 18mo. 4s.

# MODERN LANGUAGES.

## French.

**BARRÈRE (A.)** PROFESSOR, R.M.A. Woolwich.

────── RÉCITS MILITAIRES. Selections from modern French authors, with short biographical introductions in French, and English notes for the use of army students and others. Crown 8vo. 3s.

────── PRÉCIS OF COMPARATIVE FRENCH GRAMMAR AND IDIOMS, and Guide to Examinations. Cloth. *Second edition, revised*, 3s. 6d.

────── JUNIOR GRADUATED FRENCH COURSE affording materials for Translation, Grammar, and Conversation. Being an introduction to the Graduated French Course. Cloth, 1s. 6d.

────── ELEMENTS OF FRENCH GRAMMAR AND FIRST STEPS IN IDIOMS. With numerous Exercises and a Vocabulary, being an Introduction to the Précis of Comparative French Grammar. Crown 8vo. cloth, 2s.

**BELLENGER'S** MODERN FRENCH CONVERSATION. Containing Elementary Phrases and New Easy Dialogues, in French and English, on the most familiar subjects. 12mo. 2s. 6d.

**BOSSUT'S** FRENCH WORD BOOK. 18mo. 1s.

────── FRENCH PHRASE BOOK. 18mo. 1s.

**BOWER.** PUBLIC EXAMINATION FRENCH READER. With a Vocabulary to every extract, suitable for all Students who are preparing for a French Examination. By A. M. Bower, F.R.G.S., late Master in University College School, &c. Cloth, 3s. 6d.

"The book is a very practical and useful one, and it must prove very handy for students who are preparing for a French examination, the persons for whose special aid it has been specially provided. It would also serve admirably for use in schools as a class book."— *Schoolmaster.*

**DELILLE'S** FRENCH GRAMMAR. In Two Parts. I.—Accidence. II.—Syntax, written in French, with Exercises conducive to the speaking of the French Language, &c. 12mo. 5s. 6d. Key, 3s.

────── EASY FRENCH POETRY FOR BEGINNERS; or, Short Selections in Verse on a Graduated Plan for the Memory. With English Notes. 12mo. 2s.

**DELILLE'S** MODÈLES DE POÉSIE FRANÇAIS. With Treatise on French Versification. *New edition.* 12mo. 6s.

────── RÉPERTOIRE DES PROSATEURS FRANCAIS. With Biographical Sketches, &c. *New edition.* 12mo. 6s. 6d.

────── MANUEL ÉTYMOLOGIQUE; or, an Interpretative Index of the most recurrent Words in the French Language. 12mo. 2s. 6d.

────── BEGINNER'S OWN FRENCH BOOK. Being a Practical and Easy Method of Learning the Elements of the French Language. 12mo. cloth, 2s. Key, 2s,

**DES CARRIÈRES'** FRENCH IDIOMATICAL PHRASES AND FAMILIAR DIALOGUES. Square, 3s. 6d.

**DES CARRIÈRES'** HISTOIRE DE FRANCE, DEPUIS L'ETABLISSEMENT DE LA MONARCHIE. Continuée jusqu'au rétablissement de l'Empire sous Napoleon III., par C. J. Delille. 12mo. 7s.

**DUVERGER'S** COMPARISON BETWEEN THE IDIOMS, GENIUS, AND PHRASEOLOGY OF THE FRENCH AND ENGLISH LANGUAGES. *New edition.* 12mo. 4s. 6d.

**GASC (F. E. A.)** AN IMPROVED MODERN POCKET DICTIONARY OF THE FRENCH AND ENGLISH LANGUAGES. *New edition.* 16mo. cloth, 2s. 6d. Also in 2 vols. in neat leatherette, 5s.

—— MODERN FRENCH-ENGLISH AND ENGLISH-FRENCH DICTIONARY. *New edition, revised.* In 1 vol. 8vo. 10s. 6d.

**HAMEL'S** NEW UNIVERSAL FRENCH GRAMMAR. *New Edition.* 12mo. 4s.

—— GRAMMATICAL EXERCISES UPON THE FRENCH LANGUAGE. *New edition.* 12mo. 4s. Key, 3s.

—— FRENCH GRAMMAR AND EXERCISES. *New edition.* 12mo. 5s. 6d. Key, 4s.

**LEVIZAC'S** DICTIONARY OF THE FRENCH AND ENGLISH LANGUAGES. *New edition*, by N. Lambert. 12mo. 6s. 6d.

**NUGENT'S** POCKET DICTIONARY OF THE FRENCH AND ENGLISH LANGUAGES. *New edition*, revised by J. C. J. Tarver. *Pearl edition*, 4s. 6d.

**OLLENDORFS (Dr. H. G.)** NEW METHOD OF LEARNING TO READ, WRITE, AND SPEAK A LANGUAGE IN SIX MONTHS. Adapted to the French. *New edition.* 12mo. 6s. 6d. Key, 8vo. 7s.

**PRACTICAL COMMERCIAL CORRESPONDENCE.** *See Miscellaneous.*

## Whittaker's French Series.

For the use of Schools and Private Students. Edited by A. Barrère, Prof. R.M.A. Woolwich, &c., and others. Each number with a literary Introduction and Arguments in English, foot-notes explaining the more difficult passages, and translations of the idiomatic expressions into the corresponding English idioms.

Fcap. 8vo, each number, sewed, 6*d*. ; cloth, 9*d*.

*Now Ready:—*
1. SCRIBE. LE VERRE D'EAU. Barrère.
2. MOLIERE. LE BOURGEOIS GENTILHOMME. Gasc.
3. MOLIERE. L'AVARE. Gasc.
4. SOUVESTRE. SOUS LA TONNELLE. Desages.
5. MOLIERE. LE MISANTHROPE. Gasc.
6. GALLAND. ALI BABA. Clare.
7. CORNEILLE. LE CID. Gasc.
8, 9. LAMARTINE. JEANNE D'ARC. Barrère.
10, 11. PIRON. LA METROMANIE. Delbos.

*Others to follow.*

## Whittaker's French Classics, with English Notes.

*Fcap. 8vo. cloth.*

**AVENTURES DE TELEMAQUE.** Par Fénélon. *New edition.* Edited and revised by C J. Delille. 2*s.* 6*d.*

**HISTOIRE DE CHARLES XII.** Par Voltaire. *New edition.* Edited and revised by L. Direy. 1*s.* 6*d.*

**PICCIOLA.** Par X. B. Saintine. *New edition.* Edited and revised by Dr. Dubuc. 1*s.* 6*d.*

**SELECT FABLES OF LA FONTAINE.** *New edition.* Edited by F. Gasc, M.A. 1*s.* 6*d.*

## Whittaker's Series of Modern French Authors.

*WITH INTRODUCTION AND NOTES.*

*For Beginners.*

**LA BELLE NIVERNAISE.** Histoire d'un vieux bateau et de son équipage. By Alphonse Daudet. With 6 illustrations. Edited by James Boïelle, Senior French Master at Dulwich College. 2s. 6d. [*Ready.*

*For Advanced Students.*

**BUG JARGAL.** By Victor Hugo. Edited by James Boïelle, Senior French Master at Dulwich College. 3s. Others to follow. [*Ready.*

## German.

**FLÜGEL'S** COMPLETE DICTIONARY OF THE GERMAN AND ENGLISH LANGUAGES. Comprising the German and English, and English and German. Adapted to the English Student, with great Additions and Improvements. By C. A. Feiling, A. Heimann, and J. Oxenford. *New edition.* 2 vols. 8vo. 1l. 1s.

—— ABRIDGED GERMAN AND ENGLISH, AND ENGLISH AND GERMAN DICTIONARY. Carefully compiled from the larger Dictionary. By C. A. Feiling and J. Oxenford. *New edition.* Royal 18mo. 6s.

**GRENFELL'S** ELEMENTARY GERMAN EXERCISES. Part I. Adapted to the Rugby School German Accidence. 12mo. 1s. 6d.

**OLLENDORFF'S** (Dr. H. S.). NEW METHOD OF LEARNING TO READ, WRITE, AND SPEAK A LANGUAGE IN SIX MONTHS. Adapted to the German. *New edition.* Crown 8vo. 7s. Key, 8vo. 7s.

## Classical and Educational Works. 23

**SHELDON (E.S.) A SHORT GERMAN GRAMMAR FOR HIGH SCHOOLS AND COLLEGES.** Crown 8vo. 3s.

**WHITTAKER'S COURSE OF MODERN GERMAN.** By F. Lange, Ph.D., Professor, R.M.A. Woolwich, Examiner in German to the College of Preceptors, London; Examiner in German at the Victoria University, Manchester, and J. F. Davis, M.A., D.Lit. Extra fcap. 8vo. cloth.

**A CONCISE GERMAN GRAMMAR.** With especial reference to Phonology, Comparative Philology, English and German Correspondences, and Idioms. By Frz. Lange, Ph.D., Professor at the Royal Military Academy, Woolwich. In three Parts. Part I., Elementary, 2s. Part II., Intermediate, 2s. Part III. complete.

**ELEMENTARY GERMAN READER.** A Graduated Collection of Readings in Prose and Poetry. With English Notes and a Vocabulary. By F. Lange, Ph.D. 1s. 6d.

**ADVANCED GERMAN READER.** A Graduated Collection of Readings in Prose and Poetry. With English Notes and a Vocabulary. By F. Lange, Ph.D. and J. F. Davis, M.A., D.Lit. [*Nearly ready.*

**PROGRESSIVE GERMAN EXAMINATION COURSE.** In Three Parts. By F. Lange, Ph.D., Prof. R.M.A., Woolwich, Examiner in German to the College of Preceptors.

Comprising the Elements of German Grammar, an Historical Sketch of the Teutonic Languages, English and German Correspondences, Materials for Translation, Dictation, Extempore, Conversation and complete Vocabularies.

1. ELEMENTARY COURSE. Cloth, 2s.
2. INTERMEDIATE COURSE. Cloth, 2s.
3. ADVANCED COURSE. Second revised edition. Cloth, 1s. 6d.

"We cordially commend it as a useful help to examiners, who will find it well adapted to their needs."—*Practical Teacher.*

## German Classics, with English Notes.

*Fcap. 8vo. cloth.*

**GERMAN BALLADS.** From Uhland, Goethe, and Schiller. With Introductions to each Poem, copious Explanatory Notes, and Biographical Notices. By C. Bielefeld. 1s. 6d.

**GOETHE'S** HERMANN AND DOROTHEA. With Short Introduction, Argument, and Notes Critical and Explanatory. By Ernest Bell and E. Wölfel. 1s. 6d.

**SCHILLER'S** MAID OF ORLEANS. With Introduction and Notes. By Dr. Wagner. 1s. 6d.

―――― MARIA STUART. With Introduction and Notes. By V. Kastner, M.A. 1s. 6d.

―――― WALLENSTEIN. Complete Text. *New edition.* With Notes, Arguments, and an Historical and Critical Introduction. By C. A. Buchheim, Professor, Ph.D., 5s. Or separately—Part I.—THE LAGER AND DIE PICCOLOMINI. 2s. 6d. Part II.—WALLENSTEIN'S TOD. 2s. 6d.

## Whittaker's Series of Modern German Authors.

*With Introduction and Notes. Edited by F. Lange, Ph.D., Professor, Royal Military Academy, Woolwich.*

The attention of the heads of Colleges and Schools is respectfully directed to this new Series of "MODERN GERMAN AUTHORS" which is intended to supply the much-felt want of suitable Reading Books for English Students of German who have passed through the preliminary stages of fables and anecdotes.

To those who wish to extend their linguistic and grammatical

## Classical and Educational Works. 25

knowledge, these volumes will afford, in one respect, a great advantage over those of an earlier period, presenting, as they do, the compositions of the best living, or only recently deceased authors. The Notes, besides etymological and other explanations, will contain many useful idiomatic expressions suggested by the text, and worth committing to memory.

### FIRST SERIES.

FOR BEGINNERS. Edited, with a Grammatical Introduction, Notes, and a Vocabulary, by F. Lange, Ph.D., Professor, R.M.A. Woolwich, Examiner in German to the College of Preceptors, and H. Hager, Ph.D., Examiner in German to the London University.

HEY'S FABELN FÜR KINDER. Illustrated by O. Speckter. Edited, with an Introduction, Grammatical Summary, Words, and a complete Vocabulary. By F. Lange, Ph.D., Professor. 1s. 6d.

THE SAME, with a Phonetic Introduction, Phonetic Transcription of the Text. By F. Lange, Professor, Ph.D. 2s.

### SECOND SERIES.

FOR INTERMEDIATE STUDENTS. Edited, with a Biographical Introduction, Notes, and a complete vocabulary, by F. Lange, Ph.D., Professor, and H. Hager, Ph.D.

DOKTOR WESPE. Lustspiel in fünf Aufzügen von JULIUS RODERICH BENEDIX. Edited by F. Lange, Ph.D., Professor. 2s. 6d.

SCHILLER'S JUGENDJAHRE. Erzählung von FRZ. HOFFMANN. Edited by H. Hager, Ph.D., Professor. [*In the press.*

### THIRD SERIES.

FOR ADVANCED STUDENTS. Edited, with a Literary Introduction and Notes, by F. Lange, Ph.D., Professor, R.M.A. Woolwich, in co-operation with F. Storr, B.A. ; A. A. Macdonell, M.A. ; H. Hager, Ph.D. ; C. Neuhaus, Ph.D. and others.

MEISTER MARTIN, der Küfner. Erzählung von E. T. A. Hoffman. Edited by F. Lange, Ph.D., Professor, Royal Military Academy, Woolwich. 1s. 6d.

HANS LANGE. Schauspiel von Paul Heyse. Edited by A. A. Macdonell, M.A., Ph.D., Taylorian Teacher, University, Oxford. 2s.

AUF WACHE. Novelle von Berthold Auerbach. DER GEFRORENE KUSS. Novelle von Otto Roquette. Edited by A. A. Macdonell, M.A. 2s.

DER BIBLIOTHEKAR. Lustspiel von G. von Moser. Edited by F. Lange, Ph.D. Second revised Edition. 2s.

EINE FRAGE. Idyll von George Ebers. Edited by F. Storr, B.A., Chief Master of Modern Subjects in Merchant Taylor's School. 2s.

DIE JOURNALISTEN. Lustspiel von Gustav Freytag. Edited by Professor F. Lange, Ph.D. Second revised Edition. 2s. 6d.

ZOPF UND SCHWERT. Lustspiel von Karl Gutzkow. Edited by Professor F. Lange, Ph.D. 2s. 6d.

GERMAN EPIC TALES IN PROSE. I. Die Nibelungen, von A. F. C. Vilmar.—II. Walther und Hildegund, von Albert Richter. Edited by Karl Neuhaus, Ph.D., the International College, Isleworth. 2s. 6d.

## Italian.

**BARETTI'S** DICTIONARY OF THE ENGLISH AND ITALIAN LANGUAGES. To which is prefixed an Italian and English Grammar. *New Edition*, entirely rewritten. By G. Comelati and J. Davenport. 2 vols. 8vo. 1l. 1s.

**GRAGLIA'S** NEW POCKET DICTIONARY OF THE ITALIAN AND ENGLISH LANGUAGES. With considerable Additions, and a Compendious Elementary Italian Grammar. 18mo. 4s. 6d.

**OLLENDORFF'S (DR. H. G.)** NEW METHOD OF LEARNING TO READ, WRITE, AND SPEAK A LANGUAGE IN SIX MONTHS. Adapted to the Italian. *New Edition.* Crown 8vo. 7s. Key, 8vo. 7s.

**SOAVE'S** NOVELLE MORALI. *New Edition.* 12mo. 4s.

**VENERONI'S** COMPLETE ITALIAN GRAMMAR. By P. Rosteri. 12mo. 6s.

**VERGANI AND PIRANESI'S** ITALIAN AND ENGLISH GRAMMAR. With Exercises, &c. By J. Guichet. *New edition*, by Signor A. Tommasi. 12mo. 5s. Key, 3s.

## Russian.

**DOLBESHOFF (E.)** A DICTIONARY OF THE RUSSIAN AND ENGLISH LANGUAGES. In two volumes. Vol. I. Russian-English. Vol. II. English-Russian. Compiled by E. Dolbeshoff in co-operation with C. E. Turner, Professor of English Language and Literature at the University, St. Petersburg. [*Preparing.*]

## Spanish.

**NEUMAN AND BARETTI'S** SPANISH AND ENGLISH, AND ENGLISH AND SPANISH DICTIONARY. Revised and enlarged by M. Seoane, M.D. 2 vols. 8vo. 1l. 8s.

—— POCKET DICTIONARY. Spanish and English, and English and Spanish. Compiled from the larger work. 18mo. 5s.

**OLLENDORFF'S (DR. H. G.)** NEW METHOD OF LEARNING TO READ, WRITE, AND SPEAK A LANGUAGE IN SIX MONTHS. Adapted to the Spanish. *New edition*. 8vo. 12s. Key, 8vo. 7s.

**PONCE DE LEON'S** ENGLISH-SPANISH TECHNOLOGICAL DICTIONARY. 8vo. 1l. 16s. *See page* 31.

## Practical Mercantile Correspondence.

A Collection of Commercial Letters and Forms, with Notes, Explanatory and Grammatical, and a Vocabulary of Commercial Terms, edited by L. Simon, Chr. Vogel, Ph.D., H. P. Skelton, W. C. Wrankmore, Leland Mason, and others. Intended as Class Books for Schools and for Self-Instruction.

*Now Ready, crown 8vo, cloth:*
ENGLISH, with German Notes, 3s.
GERMAN, with English Notes, 3s.
ENGLISH, with French Notes, 4s. 6d.
FRENCH, with English Notes, 4s. 6d.

This new Collection of Model Letters and Epistolary Forms embraces the whole sphere of Commercial Transactions. Each example is provided with such remarks and explanations, that any one with a fair grammatical knowledge of the particular language will find it an easy matter to prepare a well-expressed letter.

## The Specialist's Series.

*A New Series of Handbooks for Students and Practical Engineers. Crown 8vo. With many Illustrations.*

**GAS ENGINES.** Their Theory and Management. By William Macgregor. With 7 Plates. Crown 8vo. pp. 245, 8s. 6d.

**BALLOONING:** A Concise Sketch of its History and Principles. From the best sources, Continental and English. By G. May. With Illustrations. Crown 8vo. pp. vi.-97, 2s. 6d.

**ELECTRIC TRANSMISSION OF ENERGY,** and its Transformation, Subdivision, and Distribution. A Practical Handbook by Gisbert Kapp, C.E., Associate Member of the Institution of Civil Engineers, &c. With 119 Illustrations. Crown 8vo. pp. xi.-331. *Second Edition.* 7s. 6d.

**ARC AND GLOW LAMPS.** A Practical Handbook on Electric Lighting. By Julius Maier, Ph.D., Assoc. Soc. Tel. Eng., &c. With 78 Illustrations. Crown 8vo. pp. viii.-376. 7s. 6d.

**ON THE CONVERSION OF HEAT INTO WORK.** A Practical Handbook on Heat-Engines. By William Anderson, M. Inst. C.E. With 64 Illustrations. Pp. viii.-254. *Second Edition.* Cr. 8vo. 6s.

**SEWAGE TREATMENT, PURIFICATION AND UTILIZATION**; A Practical Manual for the Use of Corporations, Local Boards, Officers of Health, Inspectors of Nuisances, Chemists, Manufacturers, Riparian Owners, Engineers and Ratepayers. By J. W. Slater, F.E.S., Editor of "Journal of Science." Crown 8vo. cloth, price 6s.

**THE TELEPHONE.** By W. H. Preece, F.R.S., and J. Maier, Ph.D. With numerous illustrations. Cr. 8vo. 12s. 6d.

**MANURES, OR THE PHILOSOPHY OF MANURING.** By Dr. A. B. Griffiths, F.R.S.Ed., F.C.S., Principal and Lecturer on Chemistry in the School of Science, Lincoln, &c., &c. Cr. 8vo. 7s. 6d.

**HYDRAULIC MOTORS: TURBINES AND PRESSURE MOTORS.** By George R. Bodmer, Assoc. M.Inst.C.E. 14s.

**ALTERNATING CURRENTS OF ELECTRICITY.** By Thomas H. Blakesley, M.A., M.Inst.C.E. 4s. 6d.

*In preparation.*

**GALVANIC BATTERIES.** By Professor George Forbes, M.A.

**INDUCTION COILS.** By Professor A. J. Fleming, M.A., D.Sc.

**THE DYNAMO.** By Guy C. Fricker.

*Others to follow.*

---

**NIPHER (F. E.) THEORY OF MAGNETIC MEASUREMENTS, WITH AN APPENDIX ON THE METHOD OF LEAST SQUARES.** One volume. Crown 8vo. cloth, 5s.

**PLANTÉ (G.) THE STORAGE OF ELECTRICAL ENERGY,** and Researches in the Effects created by Currents combining Quantity with High Tension. Translated from the French by Paul Bedford Elwell. With Portrait, and 89 Illustrations. 8vo. pp. vii.-268, cloth, 12s.

*Small crown 8vo. cloth. With many Illustrations.*

## Whittaker's Library of Arts, Sciences, Manufactures and Industries.

**ELECTRIC LIGHT INSTALLATIONS AND THE MANAGEMENT OF ACCUMULATORS.** A Practical Handbook by Sir David Salomons, Bart., M.A. 5th Edition, Revised and Enlarged, with 100 Illustrations. Cloth, 5s.

"To say that this book is the best of its kind would be a poor compliment, as it is practically the only work on accumulators that has been written."— *Electrical Review.*

**ELECTRICAL INSTRUMENT-MAKING FOR AMATEURS.** A Practical Handbook. By S. R. Bottone, Author of "The Dynamo," &c. With 60 Illustrations. Third edition. Cloth, 3s.

**ELECTRIC BELLS AND ALL ABOUT THEM.** A Practical Book for Practical Men. By S. R. Bottone. With more than 100 illustrations. *Second edition, revised.* Cloth, 3s.

**PRACTICAL IRON FOUNDING.** By the Author of "Pattern Making," &c., &c. Illustrated with over one hundred engravings. Cloth, 4s.

**ELECTRICAL ENGINEERING IN OUR HOMES AND WORKSHOPS.** A Practical Handbook. By Sydney F. Walker, M.Inst.C.E., M.I.E.E. 5s.

**THE PROTECTION OF BUILDINGS FROM LIGHTNING.** A Treatise on the Theory of Lightning Conductors from a Modern Point of View. Being the substance of two lectures delivered before the Society of Arts in March, 1888. By Oliver J. Lodge, LL.D., D.Sc., F.R.S., Professor of Physics in University College, Liverpool.

Published with various amplifications and additions, with the approval of the Society of Arts. [*In preparation.*

**ELECTRICAL INFLUENCE MACHINES:** Containing a full account of their historical development, their modern Forms, and their Practical Construction. By J. Gray. B.Sc. [*In the press.*

## Classical and Educational Works. 31

**METAL TURNING.** By J. A., author of
"Practical Ironfounding," &c. [*In the press.*
*Others in preparation.*

## Technological Dictionaries.

### ENGLISH AND GERMAN.

**WERSHOVEN (F. J.) TECHNOLOGICAL DICTIONARY OF THE PHYSICAL, MECHANICAL, AND CHEMICAL SCIENCES.** English and German. 2 vols. cloth, 5*s*.

### ENGLISH—SPANISH.

**PONCE DE LEON. TECHNOLOGICAL DICTIONARY.** English-Spanish and Spanish-English. Containing Terms employed in the Applied Sciences, Industrial Arts, Mechanics, Fine Arts, Metallurgy, Machinery, Commerce, Ship-building and Navigation, Civil and Military Engineering, Agriculture, Railway Construction, Electro-technics, &c.

Vol. I.—English-Spanish. 8vo. bound, £1 16*s*.

Vol. II.—Spanish-English. [*In preparation.*

*Post 8vo.* 814 *pp.* 10*s*. 6*d*.

**HOBLYN'S DICTIONARY OF TERMS USED IN MEDICINE AND COLLATERAL SCIENCES.** 11*th edition.* Revised throughout, with numerous Additions. By John A P. Price, B.A., M.D. Oxon., Assistant-Surgeon to the Royal Berkshire Hospital.

This new edition has undergone complete revision and emendation. Many terms, fallen more or less into disuse, have been omitted; and a considerable amount of fresh matter has been introduced, in order to meet the requirements of the present day.

1 vol. demy 4to. with 25 Double and 40 Single Plates, £2 10s.
## TECHNICAL SCHOOL AND COLLEGE BUILDING.
*Being a Treatise on the Design and Construction of Applied Science and Art Buildings, and their suitable Fittings and Sanitation.*

WITH A CHAPTER ON TECHNICAL EDUCATION.

By EDWARD COOKWORTHY ROBINS, F.S.A.

OUTLINE OF CONTENTS.—Introduction—English and Foreign Technical Education—Analysis of the Second Report of the Royal Commissioners on Technical Education—Buildings for Applied Science and Art Instruction, with examples of Foreign and English Buildings—Analysis of the Fittings necessary for these Buildings—British and Foreign Examples of the Details of the Fittings—Heating and Ventilation generally—Heating and Ventilation necessary for Applied Science and Instruction Buildings—The Planning of Buildings for Middle Class Education—Sanitary Science—Appendix.

*Full prospectus post free on application.*

"It will prove an indispensable work of reference to architects, builders, and managers of technical schools."—*Spectator.*
"A most valuable contribution to architectural literature."—*British Architect.*

---

## THE CHEMICAL ANALYSIS OF IRON.
A Complete Account of all the Best Known Methods for the Analysis of Iron, Steel, Ores, &c.

By A. A. BLAIR, Chief Chemist, U.S. Geological Survey, &c.

Royal 8vo. 14s.

---

*Second Edition, Revised.*

THE
## WORKING AND MANAGEMENT OF AN ENGLISH RAILWAY.
By GEORGE FINDLAY,

*General Manager of the London and North-Western Railway.*

WITH NUMEROUS ILLUSTRATIONS.

Crown 8vo. 7s. 6d.

---

CHISWICK PRESS:—C. WHITTINGHAM AND CO., TOOKS COURT, CHANCERY LANE.

www.ingramcontent.com/pod-product-compliance
Lightning Source LLC
Chambersburg PA
CBHW021947160426
**43195CB00011B/1251**